Idioms in practice

Jennifer Seidl

Illustrations by Timothy Jaques

Oxford University Press
1982

Oxford University Press
Walton Street, Oxford OX2 6DP

London Glasgow New York Toronto
Delhi Bombay Calcutta Madras Karachi
Kuala Lumpur Singapore Hong Kong Tokyo
Nairobi Dar Es Salaam Cape Town Salisbury
Melbourne Auckland

and associates in
Beirut Berlin Ibadan Mexico City Nicosia

ISBN 0 19 432769 8

© Oxford University Press 1982

Set in Linotron Sabon and Gill by
Tradespools Ltd, Frome, Somerset

Printed in Hong Kong

Contents

Introduction

Idioms in Practice has been written for adolescent and adult learners who wish to widen their knowledge of idiomatic English. The book aims to encourage and enliven the use of idiomatic expression, as well as to teach and test this highly important aspect of the language.

The book contains a variety of exercises, with the emphasis on achieving understanding and familiarity through the student's producing or explaining the appropriate idiom from his own resources, as a response to or comment on a contextualized situation. There are exercises on idioms using verbs, idioms using adjectives and nouns, idioms using prepositions and adverbs, comparisons and proverbs. Particular attention has been paid to phrasal verbs and idioms from special situations and categories. The language of the exercises is neutral or informal. A large proportion of business English is also included.

The organization of the book is based on the chapter-arrangement of Seidl & McMordie: *English Idioms and how to use them* (OUP 1978), and all the idioms dealt with are to be found in that volume. However, *Idioms in Practice* can be used equally well as a classwork or self-study companion to *English Idioms*, or as a teaching/learning tool in its own right. An answer key is provided.

Idioms using verbs

Complete the sentences by choosing the correct idiom.

Example
I'm used to Fred doing crazy things, but this last escapade beats the lot!
He must be absolutely _____ !

in a flutter   off one's head   off the beam
off his head

1   It's _____ that we'll win the French Ministry contract, so we'd better not send all the stock to Japan.
   on the cards   in the air   out of the question

2   'What's wrong with Mike these days? He's so nervous and irritable – always _____ .'
   on edge   in deep water   on the rocks

3   'Dorothy didn't tell me that she and Nigel were engaged.' – 'No, I didn't know about it either. I was just as much _____ as you were.'
   in the swim   in the dark   under a cloud

4   I've never seen Marjorie looking so happy. She loves her new job in the nursery school. She's really _____ when she's working with children.
   in the clouds   in good hands   in her element

5   'Are you sure that Bob's really telling you the truth? I've never been able to believe that he's _____ .'
   on the level   on the dot   on the shelf

Exercise 2 **be**

Complete the sentences by adding the correct preposition, chosen from
the list, to the idiom in *italics*.

on   off   in   at

Example
'Why's Jane so disorganized, always running around _____ *a flat spin*,
never knowing what to do?'
in

1 Sid's _____ *the doghouse* again. His wife discovered that he lost £100
   in racing bets in the last month.
2 I feel sorry for Mrs Leech. There's been so much illness in her family
   for so long that she's now _____ *her wits' end*.
3 'What on earth's wrong with Stewart?' – 'He's expecting a telephone
   call from the Director – he applied for that management job and has
   been _____ *tenterhooks* all morning.'
4 'All right, I'll tell you, but remember it's still unofficial – strictly _____
   the record!'
5 It's _____ *the cards* that the Liberals will win the election. The polls
   say that the voters think that the Conservatives are only interested in
   serving Big Business.

Exercise 3   **be**

Complete the conversation by choosing the correct idiom from the list.

on the dole	*up to the mark*
on tour	*off the map*
at someone's beck and call	*on the beat*
in one's line	*on call*
out of the question	

'What are you going to do when you leave school? Do you still want to become a doctor?'

'No, that has its disadvantages – you're ＿＿ at weekends and sometimes at night. And I don't think I'd get a place to study medicine, anyway. My teacher says I'm not ＿＿ in chemistry.'

'How about journalism? I can imagine you as a top reporter.'

'Oh, no. I'd hate rushing from one place to another, always looking for news or scandal. That's completely ＿＿ .'

'What about the Civil Service?'

'No, too boring, and too much hierarchy. You're always ＿＿ , doing what you're told to do.'

'Why not join the police force?'

'Well, it may be interesting work as a detective, but I don't fancy being a constable ＿＿ for the first few years. That's not ＿＿ at all.'

'It would be a comfortable quiet life, if you lived in a tiny country village, somewhere ＿＿ .'

'Too quiet for me! I had thought of studying music and then joining an orchestra – I play the violin in my spare time. But then you're hardly ever at home, continually ＿＿ giving concerts.'

'Well, whatever you do, you'll have to start applying for jobs soon, otherwise you'll finish up ＿＿ !'

Exercise 4   **break**

Complete the sentences by choosing the correct idiom from the list.

break the back of something   *break the ice*
break someone's fall   *break fresh ground*
break the bank   *break the news*

Example
Jimmy fell down the apple tree yesterday. Luckily, the hedge _____ ,
otherwise he might have been hurt badly.
broke his fall

1 'Old Mrs Johnson's dog has been knocked down by a lorry. She
   doesn't know about it yet. Her neighbour's going to _____ .'
2 'That's the last time I'll go to a casino! I didn't expect to _____ but I
   did expect to win a pound or two!'
3 'How was Sarah's party?' – 'Oh, boring at the beginning, until Mark
   managed to _____ by talking about a film that most people had seen.'
4 Professor Hartmann's a prominent bio-chemist. Apparently he's
   working on a project which is expected to _____ in genetics, but it's
   being kept secret at the moment.
5 'How are you getting on with learning Spanish?' – 'Oh, I've _____ the
   grammar, but it's the vocabulary that's the problem now.'

Exercise 5   **bring**

Explain the meanings of the idioms in *italics*.

Example
All our plans will collapse if Ray now decides not to work with us. We
must think of a way of *bringing him into line*.
persuading him to agree with us

1 'How was the variety concert?' – 'Not bad at all. Jimmy Star – the
   comedian – was incredibly funny. He *brought the house down*!'

2 The police have *brought some new facts to light* in the Lord Beacon case. Apparently on the night of the murder his wife made a phone-call to Panama.

3 I wish Julia would take her career more seriously. I've tried to persuade her to work harder, but I just can't *bring* the importance of it *home to her*.

4 'Don't you remember visiting Porlock, that pretty little village in Devon? Surely you do!' – 'No, I'm afraid I can't *bring it to mind* at the moment.'

5 'Here come the runners at last! I can just see them – Shirley's in front, and there's poor Maggie, *bringing up the rear*, as usual.'

Exercise 6   come

Complete the sentences by choosing the correct idiom from the list.

come to light   *come to a head*
come into fashion   *come into force*
come down to earth *come in handy for*

Example
Don't throw these old trousers away. They'll _____ doing the gardening in.'
come in handy for

1 When do the new traffic laws _____ ?

2 'Since hard rock music _____ my house is so noisy that the cat has left home. I think I'll join him in the greenhouse!'

3 The police haven't solved the murder yet, but they're convinced that the really important facts of the case will soon _____ .

4 The tense situation _____ when Fantasian troops crossed the Utopian border.

5 'Celia's still dreaming of becoming a famous actress. She says she's waiting to be 'discovered'. It's about time she _____ and started thinking realistically about her prospects as a bank clerk.'

Exercise 7   do

Explain the meanings of the idioms in *italics*.

Example
Come to Oxford for a weekend and we'll *do the sights* together.
visit all the interesting places

1 'Joe sold Mac his car, knowing quite well that the engine was in a bad
  state and would soon break down completely.' – 'What a mean trick
  of him to *do the dirty on* Mac like that!'
2 'How's my steak coming along? I'm so hungry!' – 'You'll enjoy it.
  Look, it's *done to a turn*.'
3 'How's your cough?' – 'Much better, thanks. My doctor gave me
  some pills, and they're *doing wonders*.'
4 My typewriter was making strange noises, so I cleaned it and oiled it –
  and that *did the trick*. Now it's working perfectly again.
5 'Picnics are good fun, aren't they? Who's going to *do the honours* and
  open the wine?'

Exercise 8   fall

Explain the meanings of the idioms in *italics*.

Example
'Everyone except Derek voted to give support to the Ruritarian
refugees.' – 'Typical of him! When will he learn to *fall in line with* the
opinion of the majority?'
agree with

1 The noun 'poke' *has fallen out of use* except in the phrase 'to buy a pig
  in a poke.'
2 Diane really *fell on her feet* when she took a job with Barnes & Co.
  Only three weeks after she started working there, the chief secretary
  suddenly left, and Diane stepped into her place.

3 When Paul made a speech at Sylvia's leaving party, he expected his jokes to raise hilarious laughter, but every one of them *fell flat*, and he made a great fool of himself.

4 I'd been looking forward to the new production of King Lear, but it *fell short of my expectations*. The theatrical company turned out to be too young and inexperienced.

5 'When Stan hears that I've won two free tickets for the football final, he'll *fall over himself* to be nice to me, hoping that I'll give him one of them.'

Exercise 9   get

Substitute for each of the phrases in *italics* an idiom, chosen from the list, with the same meaning.

get on one's nerves	*get hold of the wrong end of the stick*
get the sack	*get out of bed on the wrong side*
get a move on	*get down to brass tacks*

Example
'Why doesn't Rita blow her nose? That sniff of hers really *irritates me*.'
gets on my nerves

1 'Your grandfather tells me that you've found a job in Hong Kong. When do you leave?' – 'No. I told him that a friend of mine who lives in Hong Kong is coming to visit me! It's typical of Grandad to *misunderstand things thoroughly*.'

2 'Come on Jack, *hurry up*! I can't wait here all day!'

3 Since Jim *was dismissed* from the furniture factory, he hasn't bothered to look for a new job.

4 'We haven't much time for our meeting today, so I suggest that we *start discussing the essential matters* immediately.'

5 'Donald shouted at me for no reason at all when I spoke to him just now. He must *be in a bad mood* again this morning.'

Exercise 10   give

Explain the meanings of the idioms in *italics*.

Example
I found her opinions so unreasonable and unpleasant that I just had to
give vent to my anger and disgust.
show

1 When the staff heard that some of them were to get their wage-rises
   before Christmas and others after Christmas, it *gave rise to* a lot of
   ill-feeling.
2 The police managed to follow the suspect as far as the end of the
   motorway, but then he managed to *give them the slip* by turning
   sharply into a narrow lane and disappearing into the woods.
3 I saw Betty at the post-office this morning, but for some reason she
   gave me the cold shoulder. I can't understand why, because I'm sure I
   haven't said or done anything to offend her.
4 'We wanted to give you the book as a complete surprise on your
   birthday, but I suppose Ben *gave the game away* when he asked you if
   you'd already read it.'
5 'Why is Kevin always criticizing you in front of other people? If I were
   you, I'd *give him a piece of your mind* next time he does it.'

Exercise 11   **go**

Substitute for each of the phrases in *italics* an idiom, chosen from the list, with the same meaning.

go the whole hog	*go up the wall*
go behind someone's back	*go to one's head*
go to rack and ruin	*go to town*

Example
When my father sees what I've done to his car, he'll *get extremely annoyed*!
go up the wall

1 The Bartons *spent a lot of money* decorating their daughter's room — then suddenly she decided to rent a bed-sitter in town!
2 The Jacksons have a country cottage in Kent. It's at least two hundred years old. But they're hardly ever there to look after it, so it's slowly *reaching a very bad state of repair*.
3 'You'd better tell the Sales Manager the truth about what you're planning to do. I wouldn't advise *doing it without his knowledge*.'
4 When we moved into our new house we didn't intend to rebuild the kitchen and buy new furniture as well. But Brian said we may as well *make a thorough job of it*, so we did – and plunged ourselves deep into debt!
5 'Chris's promotion has really *made him proud and conceited* – he doesn't even say "Good Morning" to me any more.'

Exercise 12   **have**

Complete the conversation by choosing the correct idiom from the list.

have a brush with someone   *have other fish to fry*
have had it   *have too many irons in the fire*
have it out with someone   *have the cheek to do something*
have one's sleep out

'I'm afraid I've just _____ with Maggie. She thinks it was me who
scraped her car in the car park, because the scratch marks were red. But I
didn't use my car on the day it happened.'

'You mean that Maggie _____ to accuse you of damaging her car, just
because your car happens to be red? That's no proof!'

'I wouldn't take it too seriously if I were you, Peter. The trouble with
Maggie is that she _____ – always trying to do too many things at the
same time. That's why she's so irritable. She was working very late again
last night and was back here by eight this morning. She probably didn't
_____ last night.'

'Yes, I suppose you're right. If I thought she meant the accusation
seriously, I'd go and _____ , but as it is, it's a waste of time trying to
reason with her. And besides, I _____ . I can't waste my time on stupid
arguments.'

'I'll talk to her and try to make her realize that you aren't the guilty
party.'

'OK, Janet, that's nice of you. But if she goes on thinking that it was
my fault, then she _____ as far as I'm concerned.

Exercise 13 **hold lay**

Explain the meanings of the idioms in *italics*.

Example
'I hope you understand that the tennis committee has *laid a serious charge against you*, John. They will not tolerate swearing during a match.
accused you of a serious offence

1 I wanted to tell my parents the truth about my sister, but then I thought it best to *hold my tongue*, as it might have created even more trouble.
2 'Tom's lost his job again.' – 'But it's the third time this year that he's been sacked! He doesn't seem able *to hold a job down* at all.'
3 'Sheila's worried about her interview with the Manager tomorrow. She's afraid he'll reject all her proposals.' – 'Oh, I wouldn't worry about Sheila. She can *hold her own* in any argument.'
4 Don't let Keith upset you. He loves *laying down the law* – but nobody takes him very seriously.
5 I thought Horton's speech about the Principal was too flattering. I agree that the college will be sorry to lose him, but Horton did *lay it on thick*, didn't he?

Exercise 14   **keep**

Complete the sentences by choosing the correct idiom.

Example
Apparently Bill Barker didn't resign, as he told us – he was sacked! He didn't want anyone to know, so he tried to _____ , but the truth had to come out some time.
keep it up   keep it dark   keep a diary
keep it dark

1 'I'm taking my exam tomorrow. Wish me luck, and don't forget to _____ for me!'
   keep at it   keep one's fingers crossed   keep going

2 The Wilsons have just bought a new car, so I expect the Fosters will soon buy a bigger and better one! In our neighbourhood it's important to _____ .
   keep the change   keep in with someone   keep up with the Joneses

3 'Who lives in the old house on the hill?' – 'A famous poet – all by himself. But I hardly ever see him. He _____ .'
   keep oneself to oneself   keep it to oneself   keep house

4 'I'm moving to London next month, but I'll _____ , I promise. Here's my new address, so that you can contact me.'
   keep in touch   keep tabs on   keep someone on

5 'I heard that Dick Doyle has gone bankrupt.' – 'I don't know whether it's true or not, but if it is, he certainly manages to _____ . Doesn't he still drive his Rolls-Royce?'
   keep fit   keep a secret   keep up appearances

Exercise 15   make

Substitute for each of the phrases in *italics* an idiom, chosen from the list, with the same meaning.

make a virtue of necessity   *make oneself felt*
make a beeline for something   *make short work of something*
make a name for oneself   *make heavy weather of something*

Example
Philip's doing very well in aeronautics. He's published a lot of research work and is on the way to *becoming famous* internationally.
making a name for himself

1 'When the children see those jam tarts they'll *eat them all up very quickly*.'
2 'Beth doesn't like the new xerox machine. She says it's too complicated.' – 'It's easy when you get used to it. But then, Beth often *treats something as more difficult than it really is*.'
3 Richard arrived late for the reception, and as soon as he'd taken off his coat he *hurried directly to* the food table, thinking there wouldn't be much left for him.
4 Jerry likes organizing people, and since he's been put in charge of the department, he's really been *using his authority*.
5 'Why's Kate working in that home for handicapped children? Did she feel she had to do something useful for society?' – 'Well actually she's just *doing good because she had to* – it's the only job she could get!'

Exercise 16   play

Explain the meanings of the idioms in *italics*.

Example
If I'm late, try and *play for time* by saying that you want to read the reports before starting the meeting.
gain extra time

1 Jim Carter won't *play ball with you* unless you agree to split the profits with him 50-50.

2 'I refuse to *play second fiddle to you* all my life! I want my own career! I want my own bank account!'

3 I don't think it's fair of Brenda to treat Chris the way she does. She's not really seriously interested in him – she's just *playing fast and loose* with him until she finds someone she likes better.

4 Norman's a very intelligent fellow. If he *plays his cards right*, he may end up a partner in the firm before he's 40.

5 Take my advice and don't hand in your resignation, however bitter you may feel. That's exactly what Briggs is hoping you will do. You would be *playing into his hands*.

Exercise 17 **pull**

Explain the meanings of the idioms in *italics*.

Example
Be very careful when you're working with Rodney. Make sure you check all his calculations, because he'll try to *pull a fast one* if he thinks he can manage it.
deceive you

1 Don't let the estate agent *pull the wool over your eyes* when he shows you the old house. He'll probably tell you it's in excellent repair even if it's got dry rot, woodworm, rising damp and sinking foundations.

2 'Don't take Des seriously. He was only *pulling your leg* – and certainly didn't think you'd be offended.'

3 'If you intend passing the exam, you'll have to *pull your socks up*! You've done no work at all for the last three months.'

4 If everybody *pulls their weight*, we'll achieve our production target.

5 Simon's used to *pulling strings* to get exactly what he wants. If he didn't know so many influential people, he would never have reached the position he's in now.

Exercise 18   put

Substitute for each of the phrases in *italics* an idiom, chosen from the list, with the same meaning.

put one's foot in it   *put someone in the picture*
put the cart before the horse   *put two and two together*
put one's foot down   *put the screws on someone*

Example
I didn't realize that you hadn't told the boss that you intend to leave the firm. I'm afraid I *made an embarrassing mistake* when I mentioned it to him. I'm very sorry.
put my foot in it

1 Victor obviously doesn't know what's happened, otherwise he wouldn't have made such a tactless remark. You'd better *tell him what the situation is.*

2 I understand that you've employed a builder before seeing an estimate. Isn't that *doing things in the wrong order?*

3 'The bank has refused to give the firm a further loan unless we change our policy.' – 'Oh, so that's how it is! I knew they'd *try to force us to do what they want* – they've never approved of the way we've been running the firm.'

4 Nobody has actually told me that Bob and Nigel are going to end their partnership, but *drawing conclusions from the information I have*, it's clear that Nigel is planning to go into business with Roger Dunhill before the year's out.

5 'If I were you, I wouldn't tolerate such behaviour any longer. It's time you *objected firmly*, before it's too late!'

Exercise 19   **see**

Explain the meanings of the idioms in *italics*.

Example
Have you seen her passport? It shows she's visited over 50 countries. She
really must have *seen life*.
gained great experience (through travelling)

1 'Am I glad our boss is leaving! She's been so bad-tempered these last
  few months that everyone will be glad to *see the back of her*.'
2 Rachel is very happy with Robert at the moment, but when she stops
  seeing things through rose-coloured spectacles I think she'll realize
  that he's only after her money.
3 'Could you possibly *see your way clear to* drafting the report before
  the weekend? I know it's short notice, but it's extremely important.'
4 'I'm going to have a chat with the manager about general issues of
  staffing and training. But it's really only a pretence – I want to *see how
  the land lies* before I ask him for a rise.'
5 Now I'm beginning to *see the light*! You're suggesting that Holmes has
  resigned because he knows that in a few months' time the firm will be
  bankrupt, aren't you?

Exercise 20   set

Explain the meanings of the idioms in *italics*.

Example
Please *set my mind at rest* – you're not really going to marry Pam, are you?
free me from worry

1 'Can you hear that strange whining noise from the air-conditioner? It *sets my teeth on edge* and I can't concentrate.'

2 'I was surprised to hear that Gloria's got engaged to the boss's son.' – 'Oh, surely you noticed that she *set her cap at him* as soon as he started to work in the firm?'

3 The new manager's quite a hard worker, but he'll *never set the Thames on fire* – he just hasn't got enough imagination.

4 Brian made a sarcastic remark about my private life – so I told him to *set his own house in order* before criticizing me.

5 We were having a quiet discussion, until Joe asked Steve why he hadn't come to the meeting last week. Of course, that *set the ball rolling*. Steve became angry, the others took sides, and it all ended up in a furious argument.

Exercise 21 **stand**

Substitute for each of the phrases in *italics* an idiom, chosen from the list, with the same meaning.

stand one's ground   *stand a good chance of something*
stand to reason   *stand someone in good stead*
stand on ceremony   *stand clear of something*

Example
I advise you to take a course in shorthand and typing. Even if you don't want secretarial work, it'll *be a great advantage to you* for many jobs.
stand you in good stead

1 I'd say that Margaret *has good prospects* of winning the tennis tournament. She has a very strong backhand and is excellent at the net.

2 'Should I wear a dinner-jacket on Saturday evening? – 'No, the Langtons always give informal, relaxed parties. There's no need to *be very formal* – in fact some of their friends don't even wear a tie.'

3 *It's quite obvious* that Paul won't sell his business now that he's got it running so well.

4 I overheard Ann having an argument with Bill. Bill's a good talker, but Ann's well able to *maintain and defend her position*.

5 "*Keep away from* the doors!" shouted the conductor as he rang the bell.

Exercise 22   **take**

Complete the sentences by choosing the correct idiom.

Example
Tony hardly speaks to Janet when they're with other people now. He's
so used to having her around that he _____ .
take part   take someone for granted   take no notice
takes her for granted

1 Mike and Phil had an argument last night about who does most
   cleaning in the flat they're sharing. I was careful not to _____ , as I
   want to stay good friends with them both.
   take an interest   take sides   take someone's fancy

2 'Arthur has become very arrogant and over-confident since he got
   promotion. He needs _____ .'
   take heart   take heed   take someone down a peg or two

3 I'd prefer to go to university instead of going into the family business,
   which doesn't interest me much. But I'm afraid my father would
   _____ .
   take a dim view of it   take a risk   take one's word for it

4 'Don't hesitate too long and think too much about it! If you want to
   marry the girl, why don't you _____ and ask her?'
   take a hint   take the bull by the horns   take a chair

5 People often make jokes about Alfred's figure – he seems to be getting
   fatter. But he doesn't get angry or feel insulted, he _____ .
   take it easy   take the rough with the smooth   take it in good part

Exercise 23 **turn**

Substitute for each of the phrases in *italics* an idiom, chosen from the list, with the same meaning.

turn over a new leaf	*turn a deaf ear to something*
turn someone's head	*turn the corner*
turn the scales in someone's favour	*turn one's hand to anything*

Example
Bob is very good at repairing things. Whether you've got a leaking tap or an electrical fault, he can *deal with all problems.*
turn his hand to anything

1 Helen *refused to listen to* her father's advice and she's regretted it ever since.

2 A pretty blonde waitress who works in the new restaurant seems to have *attracted* John. He has lunch there every day now.

3 Phil promised his parents that he would *better himself and start again* after he was released from borstal.

4 'How's your grandfather? Someone said he had pneumonia.' – 'Yes, we were very worried about him, but he's *got over the most critical part* now, and he's going to be OK.'

5 There were two equally good candidates for the position of overseas sales representative. The fact that John speaks three foreign languages and the other candidate only one *decided the matter favourably for John.*

Exercise 24

Complete the conversation by choosing the correct idiom from the list.

be asking for trouble   *pick holes in something*
blow one's own trumpet   *rub someone up the wrong way*
butter someone up   *stick at nothing*
fly off the handle   *tell someone where to get off*

'That new supervisor's not very popular with the office staff.'
　'Oh? Why's that?'
　'Well, she's the type who'll _____ to get what she wants. She's always chatting with the manager, telling him how good he is – she _____ all the time.'
　'And how does she treat her own staff?'
　'Well, she's quite fond of _____ , telling us what a great person she is. And she's already _____ several people's work, although the previous supervisor never had reason to.'
　'It sounds to me as if she's _____ . The staff won't stand that sort of treatment for very long.'
　'You're right. Old Henry, for one, won't take criticism that easily. He's likely to _____ and _____ , because it's her way of talking to people that really _____ .'

Exercise 25

Complete the conversation by choosing the correct idiom from the list.

harp on the same string   *pick a quarrel*
leave much to be desired   *rain cats and dogs*
meet one's match   *talk shop*
meet someone half-way   *wear the trousers*

'For God's sake, Sue, you're not going to watch telly again, are you?'
   'Why not? We can't go out. Look at the weather! It's _____ !'
   'Well, that's no reason to watch telly, is it? I'm fed up with it, night after night. Why can't we do something else for a change?'
   'If you're trying to _____ , Bob, I'm not in the mood – so calm down. I know the programmes _____ , but they're not all that bad. There's a good thriller on in a minute.'
   'OK. Let's compromise. I'll _____ . You watch your thriller, then we'll go round to Pete and Linda's.'
   'Oh, no, not again! When you're with Pete, he mentions work and then all you two do is _____ . And all Linda ever does is grumble to me about Pete. She's always _____ .'
   'Well, I think poor old Pete has _____ with Linda. She certainly _____ in that marriage!'
   'Sh! Quiet! The thriller's starting!'
   'And who wears them in ours?'

Exercise 26

Complete the sentences, using an idiom containing the verb given in brackets.

Example
'I wish Paul and Simon would forget about their old quarrel. It's time they (bury) _____ and became friends again.'
themselves in their books   the hatchet   their dead
buried the hatchet

1 Someone ought to warn Max not to interfere in matters which don't concern him. If he's not careful, he'll (burn) _____ !
his boats   the candle at both ends   his fingers

2 Steve used to be easy to get along with, but since he got promoted he's started (throw) _____ . He obviously enjoys using his authority.
in the towel   his weight about   cold water on one's plans

3 Barbara's a very persuasive speaker, but when you examine her arguments, many of them are illogical. They just don't (hold) _____ .
the line   the fort   water

4 'I did buy Ken's car, after all. I tried to bring him down £100, but he wouldn't budge.' – 'I could've told you that he wouldn't reduce the price. He always (drive) _____ .'
people mad   a hard bargain   people to drink

5 'We were enjoying making plans for the exhibition. Then Alex came in and said the design of the display was too trendy.' – 'Well, it's just like Alex to (throw) _____ , isn't it?'
a fit   cold water on one's plans   his weight about

Exercise 27

Complete the sentences by choosing the correct idiom.

Example
Jeff hasn't managed to get a place at a university and can't find a job
either. I told him not to *lose* _____ , as something suitable was sure to
turn up.
his tongue   heart   his head
lose heart

1 I'd like the cheaper flight to Hong Kong, but then I wouldn't be able to
break _____ and visit the Bangkok office.
the contract   the journey   my word

2 I'm not quite sure what Jim Watson is planning. He's a very clever
businessman who never *shows* _____ until the very last minute.
fight   his cards   his teeth

3 'There's a lot of dissatisfaction about. The Director has called a
meeting so that the staff will have a chance to say what's troubling
them.' – 'That's a good idea. It's always better to *clear* _____ .'
the decks   the air   one's name

4 I still haven't worked out the best solution to the problem. I had hoped
that Gordon would *drop* _____ on how to do it, but every time I
mention it, he makes some excuse and leaves the room.
a line   a stitch   a hint

5 'Tom's threatened to break off his engagement to Christina. He
doesn't like her travelling so much and meeting so many men.' – 'It's
ridiculous to be so jealous. Why doesn't she *call* _____ ? She must
know that he's not serious.'
the banns   a halt   his bluff

Exercise 28

Complete the conversation by choosing the correct idiom from the list.

cut it fine
cut someone off with a penny
kill two birds with one stone

lead someone a dog's life
let by-gones be by-gones
pick a quarrel

'Come on, Mike! Hurry up! We're going to miss the 10.15 train!'

'But it's 10 o'clock already! That's what I call _____ . Why didn't you tell your mother that we'd be arriving later?'

'Well, I thought if we went early, we could visit Uncle Arthur as well. That would _____ and save us an extra journey.'

'You know I'm not keen on visiting Uncle Arthur. Remember last time!'

'Yes, I admit it was a disaster, but it's best to forget it and _____ . I'm sure Uncle Arthur didn't really mean to cause trouble.'

'Oh yes he did! He deliberately _____ and criticized me. I feel sorry for poor Aunt Joan – I bet he _____ .'

'Well, you know how he is. He's such a dominating personality. It's just his nature. And remember, you're his only heir.'

'Yes, and he got so furious with me that he threatened to _____ . And he can do, for all I care!'

2
Idioms using phrasal verbs

Exercise 29

Complete the sentences by adding the correct adverb, chosen from the list, to the verb in *italics*.

off   in   out   over   up   down

Our television has *broken* _____ . It's been odd for a few days – first no picture, then no sound, and now nothing at all.
broken down

1 'I don't believe Ronald lied about his expenses. He's never done anything dishonest in his life! The whole story just doesn't *add* _____ .'

2 If you promised Maggie that you'd go with her to Rome, then you'll have to. She's looked forward to it so much, and it would be mean to *back* _____ now.

3 Don't worry too much about that business. It's unpleasant at the moment, but it'll *blow* _____ and be forgotten in a few weeks' time.

4 We were having a cup of coffee and a chat when Paula *burst* _____ , laden with parcels.

5 'If you don't intend coming with us to Stratford, say so now. Don't say yes and then *cry* _____ at the last moment.'

Exercise 30   **be**

Substitute for each of the phrases in *italics* an idiom, chosen from the list, with the same meaning.

be on to someone   *be in for something*
be in on something   *be down on someone*
be up against something   *be at someone*

Example
Apart from Jean and Bob, no one else *was informed about* the arrangements.
was in on

1 Joe*'s likely to get* a nasty shock. He thinks the car repairs will only cost about £30, but they're sure to cost at least £100.

2 'Don't *be critical of* poor Sarah all the time. She hasn't been trained for this type of work, so it's not her fault if she's a bit slow.'

3 'The police seem to *be on the track of* the bank robbers, judging by this newspaper report. They've concentrated their search on a particular area.'

4 'My mother will *start nagging at me* to clean up my room when she sees the mess it's in.'

5 John has won all the local squash championships, but he'll *be confronted with* tough competition when he plays in the county championships.

Exercise 31 **break**

Complete the sentences by choosing the correct idiom from the list.

break up	*break something down*
break in	*break through something*
break something up	*break someone in*

Example
It is obvious from this article that the Suzuki company has already _____ many of the technical barriers we are meeting in developing video equipment.
broken through

1 Our new secretary's been given the simpler letters to type. The supervisor wants to _____ (her) _____ gently!

2 'Quiet! Don't keep on _____ when someone else is talking. Wait until it's your turn.'

3 There was some fighting between the men on the picket lines outside the factory. The police had to be called in to _____ (it) _____ .

4 'What time do you expect the meeting to _____ ?'

5 'The boss wants these travel expenses to be _____ still further.' – 'But that's impossible! They're already as detailed as anyone could make them.'

Exercise 32

Complete the sentences by adding the correct preposition, chosen from the list, to the verb in *italics*.

with   for   to   after   on   in

Example
You both look very healthy. This country air obviously *agrees* _____ you.
agrees with

1 'I met Bob in the supermarket yesterday and he *asked* _____ you – he wanted to know if you like the new job.'
2 'Where's the shop assistant?' – 'She's *attending* _____ a customer in the other department at the moment.'
3 I knew that it would be difficult to get my project accepted by the management, but I hadn't *bargained* _____ quite so much opposition.
4 Their new record will appeal to older listeners but I doubt if it will *catch* _____ among the younger pop fans.
5 'I hate driving on motorways when lorries *cut* _____ so dangerously.'

Exercise 33   **bring**

Substitute for each of the phrases in *italics* an idiom, chosen from the list, with the same meaning.

bring someone up   *bring something off*
bring something in   *bring something on*
bring something up   *bring someone round*

Example
There's talk of the Government *introducing* a new tax relief scheme for families with more than three children.
bringing in

1 'We shall not have time for all the topics on the agenda and I suggest we *begin a discussion on* the sales performance at the next meeting.'

2 Robert had good reason to be pleased with himself. He *completed* the deal *successfully*, although no one expected him to.

3 'I've got a bad headache. It must have been the long spell of night-driving that *caused it*. All those bright car lights dazzle me.'

4 Paul doesn't agree with our scheme, but I know how to *persuade* him.

5 My father was killed in an air-crash, leaving my mother to *rear* six children on very little money.

Exercise 34   **call**

Complete the sentences by choosing the correct idiom from the list.

call on someone   *call someone out*
call for someone   *call someone up*
call for something   *call something off*

Example
It's started to rain slightly, but I don't think that we'll have to _____ the tennis match.
call off

1 'The hospital's just rung up. Sheila's had twins!' – 'Congratulations! This _____ a celebration!'

2 'Why don't you _____ (me) _____ when you've decided whether to come. Telephone after six because I'll be out until then.'

3 The union of state employees is threatening to _____ all its members unless the Government agrees to a 24% wage-claim.

4 'You'd better ask the taxi company to arrange for someone to _____ (you) at 7 tomorrow morning.'

5 Then suddenly the chairman _____ (me) to explain the results shown on the computer print-out.

Exercise 35 come

Substitute for each of the phrases in *italics* an idiom, chosen from the list, with the same meaning.

come through	*come along*	*come to*
come up	*come across something*	*come off*

Example
Dick loves making plans, but unfortunately they never seem to *materialize*.
come off

1 We had a meeting of the committee last night. The matter of the new table tennis equipment *was discussed*, and we decided to buy three new tables.
2 'How's the report *progressing*? Have you finished it yet?'
3 'I *found* these old maps in an antique shop. They're probably worth much more than I paid for them.'
4 The first thing he did when he *regained consciousness* after the accident was to ask for a cigarette.
5 'Your posting to the New York office has just *been received* by telex!'

Exercise 36

Substitute for each of the phrases in *italics* an idiom, chosen from the list, with the same meaning.

come out with something	*fall back on something*
come up with something	*get on to someone*
drop out of something	*go down with something*
break out in something	

'Jack's wife rang – he's *got* the measles so he won't be able to help with the party.'
'Never mind. Everything seems to be organized except the glasses. But we've plenty of paper cups to *use as a reserve*.'
'But don't we need some entertainment for the kids? Who's likely to

produce some good ideas?'
    'Why don't you *contact* Mike Smith? He used to be a conjurer.'
    'I'll ring him this afternoon. But I hope more guests don't suddenly *become covered with* spots! It will be awful if everyone starts *withdrawing from* the party.'
    'What a pessimistic thing to *say*!'

Exercise 37

Complete the sentences by adding the correct adverb, chosen from the list, to the verb in *italics*.

off   up   in   over   through   down

Example
'There's a formal reception, followed by a dinner and dance, so we'll have to *dress* _____ .'
dress up

1 'I'll need a few drinks to *calm me* _____ before I make my speech at the reception.'

2 The tension will begin to *ease* _____ now that the management's agreed to consider the union's claims.

3 The Customs *went* _____ everybody's luggage. Apparently they were searching for diamonds stolen in Amsterdam this morning.

4 'Has Marjorie managed to get a full-time teaching job yet?' – 'No, she's still *filling* _____ for a friend who's in hospital.'

5 Poor Mary – she's never *got* _____ the disappointment of failing her law exams.

Exercise 38   get

Complete the sentences by choosing the correct idiom from the list.

get over something   get through
get at someone   get on
get along   get around

A rumour has _____ that the firm is in financial difficulties, but no one really believes it.
got around

1 'Stop _____ me! I know it was my fault and I've said I'm sorry!'
2 I'm very pleased to hear that your father has _____ his illness and is feeling well again.
3 'How can he _____ without money for his food during the journey?'
4 With her superb financial mind and good relationship with the factory staff she's certain to _____ as a member of management.
5 'Why are you so late?' – 'I've been trying to ring Berlin all morning and I only _____ five minutes ago.'

Exercise 39   go

Complete the sentences by choosing the correct idiom.

Example
'What's _____ next door? Can you hear that terrible noise?'
go about   go on   go by
going on

1 I was late for work this morning. I set my alarm-clock for 7.30 as usual, but for some reason it didn't _____ .
   go on   go off   go along
2 'We haven't time to finish checking the figures now, but we can _____ them after lunch.'
   go over   go into   go off

3 Cliff would like to buy a villa in Spain, but he doesn't know how best
  to ____ it. It's not simply a question of going to an estate agent.
  go over   go through   go about

4 I told my boss that it's time my salary was reviewed, as I ought to be
  earning more. He promised me that he would ____ the matter
  thoroughly.
  go about   go into   go on

5 I used to enjoy smoking, but since I saw that television programme on
  lung cancer, I've ____ it completely. I wouldn't touch one now.
  go by   go over   go off

Exercise 40

Substitute for each of the phrases in *italics* an idiom, chosen from the list,
with the same meaning.

go through with something   make up for something
burst in on something   keep on at someone
keep in with someone   put in for something

Example
If I were married to Jim's wife, I'd go mad! She *pesters him continually*
all the time.
keeps on at him

1 Sarah has always made a point of *maintaining friendly relations with*
  influential people, so she always gets what she wants.

2 Annie has never known life in a big city because she's always lived in a
  small village. But when she comes to London, she'll want to
  compensate for lost time.

3 The union have *claimed* a 20% rise in the New Year – but they aren't
  very optimistic about getting it.

4 He *suddenly interrupted* our conversation only to tell us a stupid
  rumour about one of the applicants.

5 'Does Ben intend to *conclude* the deal?' – 'He hasn't decided yet.'

Exercise 41

Complete the sentences by adding the correct preposition, chosen from
the list, to the verb in *italics*.

on   in   at   to   for   upon

Example
'I didn't like this wallpaper when I first bought it, but it's a pattern that
grows _____ you the more you see it.'
grows on

1 If anyone offered me the opportunity of travelling to India, I'd *jump*
_____ it.
2 Oxbridge & Co were surprised by the large increase in the bank rate
after borrowing so much money to rebuild the warehouse. They may
have to *settle* _____ a new extension instead.
3 'I couldn't make up my mind which coat to buy, but I finally *decided*
_____ this one with the fur collar.'
4 'I'm so excited about my promotion – I only heard this morning and it
hasn't really *sunk* _____ yet!'
5 When the police interview you about the accident, *stick* _____ the
truth – it's always safer that way.

Exercise 42   **keep**

Substitute for each of the phrases in *italics* an idiom, chosen from the list,
with the same meaning.

*keep at something   keep up with someone
keep someone up   keep on
keep in with someone   keep something up*

Example
I want to *stay friendly with* Keith Barber. He's a good lawyer, and I may
need his advice soon.
keep in with

1 If you'd *persisted with* it, you would've finished the sales report by now.

2 '*Continue* taking the medicine until your temperature is normal.'

3 'I'm sorry that I've *prevented you from going to bed*, but I thought you'd want to hear about the matter in detail.'

4 He has *maintained* his interest in microelectronics for several years and now knows a great deal about the silicon chip.

5 I enjoy walking holidays with Ann although she's so fit that it's sometimes difficult to *maintain the same rate of progress as* her.

Exercise 43 **look**

Substitute for each of the phrases in *italics* an idiom, chosen from the list, with the same meaning.

look on	*look into something*
look after someone	*look over something*
look down on someone	*look someone up*

Example
Bill leaves the children with his sister when he goes out, since he knows that they'll be properly *supervised*.
looked after

1 These invoices need to be *examined* thoroughly because the total value does not agree with the figure in the covering letter.

2 Often when there's a car accident lots of people *stand and watch*, but no one offers to help.

3 Don isn't happy at work. He feels that his colleagues *consider him to be inferior* because he's the only one without a degree.

4 There was a rumour about espionage activities in Peru so counter-intelligence is *investigating* the matter very thoroughly.

5 '*Come and visit me* when you're in Brazil next year.'

Exercise 44   **hold**

Complete the sentences by choosing the correct idiom from the list.

hold something back   *hold something over*   *hold with something*
hold off   *hold out*   *hold out for something*

Example
'I don't _____ computerized records at all. Traditional book-keeping methods will prove their worth in the long run. Just wait and see!'
hold with

1 'Look at those black clouds over there. I hope the rain will _____ until the game's over.'
2 John has all the facts I need, but he won't give them to me. He's purposely _____ information _____ .
3 The car engine started making very strange noises, but thankfully it managed to _____ until I got home.
4 I don't think the union will accept an 8% wage-rise. They'll _____ much more – they're in a very aggressive mood.
5 'I strongly recommend that we _____ a discussion on item 5 until the next meeting when we shall have the monthly sales figures.'

Exercise 45

Complete the conversation by adding the correct preposition, chosen from the list.

to on off of up over out

'Can I help you, sir?'
    'I'd like to buy a new camera. The problem is that I have this old one to get rid _____ .'
    'May I see it? Yes, the case is very worn but otherwise it seems in good condition. Which model do you like?'
    'The new Japanese 35mm one which came _____ about six months ago.'

'Oh. You mean this one. Well if you buy, it I would be prepared to knock _____ £10 in exchange for your old camera. That's a 15% reduction.'

'Can I think it _____ and ring you _____ later this week? I have to work _____ my mother to lend me the money. Otherwise, I'll have to stick _____ this one for the rest of the summer.'

'Fine. I'll expect a call from you, then. Goodbye.'

'Goodbye, and thank you.'

Exercise 46

Complete the sentences by adding the correct preposition, chosen from the list, to the verb in *italics*.

on   at   over   about   in   to

Example
'Don't *sneeze* _____ John's offer – you can't be sure that anyone else will offer you something better.'
at

1 'I'll have to work late tonight, Tom. I've so much correspondence to *see* _____ and I'll be out of the office tomorrow.'

2 I was *thinking* _____ buying a video-recorder but they're so expensive.

3 *Think* my offer _____ and let me know if you're likely to accept it.

4 You won't need to go into detail about the costs when you write your report. Just *touch* _____ them in the financial section.

5 'We could give a party for Jane and Mary on your birthday – it would *tie* _____ very well and save all of us a lot of money.'

Exercise 47   **make**

Substitute for each of the phrases in *italics* an idiom, chosen from the list, with the same meaning.

make something over   make out   make something out
make something up   make off   make someone out

Example
'Janet's been behaving very strangely lately. I just can't *understand her*.'
make her out

1 'How did you *manage* at your interview? Do you think you'll get the job?'

2 If I were you, I wouldn't believe all those stories – old Bill loves *inventing things*.

3 'Have you heard the news about Mr Smith? He's *transferred* all his shares to his son which virtually gives him a place on the board!'

4 'What's wrong with Jerry? As soon as he caught sight of me this morning, he *hurried away* in the opposite direction! Or is there something wrong with me?

5 'Did you write down the number of the car?' – 'No, I couldn't *distinguish* it. It was too far away.'

Exercise 48

Complete the sentences by adding the correct adverb to the verb in
italics.

Example
If John's business deal *pays* _____ , he'll be rid of all his financial
worries.
in   off   over
off

1 'My boss has just come into the office, so I'll have to *ring* _____ now.
 We aren't allowed to make private phone calls at work.'
 up   in   off

2 I don't worry about not having any money. It'll start *rolling* _____ as
 soon as I open my new business – just you wait and see.
 off   in   away

3 If I *sold* _____ now I could buy a cottage in the country. I'll be too old
 to run the business in a few years' time, anyway.
 up   over   off

4 I don't think Ted is the type for *settling* _____ with. He's too restless
 for married life. Julie's going to regret marrying him.
 up   in   down

5 'I wish Ray wouldn't *show* _____ so much on the tennis court. Look
 how he leaps about and swings his racket to get everybody to look at
 him.'
 off   away   through

Exercise 49   put

Substitute for each of the phrases in *italics* an idiom, chosen from the list, with the same meaning.

put something off	*put up with something*
put someone up	*put something up*
put someone out	*put someone off*

Example
'Can you concentrate, or is the noise of my typewriter *distracting you*?'
putting you off

1 I've been thinking of *building* a greenhouse at the bottom of my garden – then I could grow my own tomatoes.

2 We'd be very happy to *give you accommodation* if ever you're visiting Gloucester.

3 'Please don't go to so much trouble. I really don't want to *inconvenience you*.'

4 'I'm afraid I won't be able to meet you for lunch today. Can we *postpone* it until next week?'

5 You'll have to *tolerate* the noise of the cement-mixer for a few more days.

Exercise 50

Substitute for each of the phrases in *italics* an idiom, chosen from the list, with the same meaning.

run up against something	*walk off with something*
send away for something	*stand in for someone*
take up with someone	*walk out on something*

Example
'Sheila, would you kindly *substitute for* Mary? She has a hospital appointment this morning.'
stand in for

1 Bert has grown some beautiful roses in his garden. If he enters them at the Flower Show, he'll *easily win* all the prizes.

2 I'm really surprised at the company Liz keeps these days. I never thought she'd *become friends with* such rude people.

3 We fully expected to *encounter* a certain amount of opposition, but it seems as if everybody is against the idea.

4 'Johnson's left the factory! He's just *abandoned* the project without any warning.'

5 'There's no harm in *writing a letter asking for* application forms. That won't commit you to a decision.'

Exercise 5 I   **run**

Explain the meanings of the idioms in *italics*.

Example
'If you happen to *run across* Pete, remind him that he owes me £5. I never see him these days.'
meet by chance

1 'The petrol's very low. We'd better fill up. I wouldn't like to *run out* on a country road.'

2 'Could you *run off* two hundred copies of this circular and make sure that it's distributed to all departments immediately, please?'

3 'Would you kindly *run through* my notes on the meeting and tell me if there are any mistakes?'

4 We've *run into* a few unexpected difficulties with the experiments. Gas seems to be escaping and we don't know why.

5 Don't worry so much! James probably missed the plane and can't ring you. Of course he won't be lying in a hospital bed somewhere. You're letting your imagination *run away with you*!'

Exercise 52   set

Complete the sentences by choosing the correct idiom from the list.

set something back   set about something
set in   set something up
set someone up   set off

Example
You'd better prune your roses now, before the winter weather _____ ,
otherwise you'll have to wait till the spring.
sets in

1 'We didn't expect you to arrive until after midnight. You must have
   driven at top speed. What time did you _____ ?'
2 'I would have got here sooner, but the production meeting didn't start
   until eleven o'clock and that _____ my appointments by at least an
   hour.'
3 The assembly lines have _____ new productivity records – which puts
   them in a good bargaining position for the next wage review.
4 After Michelle had finished her training and passed her exams her
   father _____ (her) _____ in her own hairdressing salon.
5 'Could you help me with this income-tax form? I don't quite know
   how to _____ it.'

Exercise 53

Complete the sentences by adding the correct adverb, chosen from the
list, to the verb in *italics*.

in   up   out   down   on   off

Example
I wonder where Pat is. She hasn't *shown* _____ yet, and it's not like her
to be late.
shown up

1 'I've had a hard day at the office and there's nothing interesting on the television so I think I'll *turn* _____ .'

2 The children loved looking after the puppy at first, but as soon as the novelty *wore* _____ , it was their mother who had to take it for walks and feed it.

3 Jill felt unhappy in her new surroundings but as time *wore* _____ she got used to everything and now she loves being there.

4 Graham has worked fantastically hard for his exams. Next week when they're over he'll be able to *wind* _____ and relax again.

5 Marilyn wanted to become a teacher, but her plans didn't *work* _____ . She couldn't get a place at college.

Exercise 54 **take**

Substitute for each of the phrases in *italics* an idiom, chosen from the list, with the same meaning.

take after someone   *take someone off*
take up something   *take to someone*
take someone on   *take someone in*

Example
'How do you like Vicky?' – 'I'm not sure that I'll ever *form a liking for her*. She seems rather arrogant and unfriendly.'
take to her

1 Bill's very popular with his work-mates – one of the reasons being that he's so good at *imitating* all the directors.

2 I didn't think Gillian would ever *form the habit of* smoking – she used to be so critical of it. Now she smokes almost a packet a day!

3 'What a bad temper that child has! Which of his parents does he *resemble*?'

4 Don't let yourself be *tricked* by people who try to sell things at the door.

5 The factory are not *employing* any new workers until their export orders improve.

Exercise 55   turn

Complete the sentences by choosing the correct idiom from the list.

turn out	*turn something down*
turn up	*turn someone off something*
turn someone away	*turn someone over*

Example
I used to love mathematics at school, until we got a teacher who was so boring that he ____ (me) ____ it completely. I've never really been interested in it since then.
turned me off

1 The Chairperson is very angry if the executive committee members ____ late for meetings.

2 Ruth wanted to be moved to another department, but when she put in an application it was ____ because her own department is understaffed.

3 'How did your steak-and-kidney pie ____ ?' – 'Not very well, unfortunately. I forgot the salt!'

4 'We've had to ____ so many people who have been queueing for tickets to watch the athletics meeting – Coe is challenging Ovett in the 1500 metres!'

5 Jim caught a burglar red-handed in his flat. The poor guy was more frightened than Jim was. He sobbed and pleaded with Jim not to ____ (him) ____ to the police.

Exercise 56   noun forms of phrasal verbs

Replace each of the phrasal verbs in *italics* with the *noun form* using the verb in brackets.

Example
Ian has a dark-room and all the necessary photographic equipment. I'll ask him to *blow up* this photo to poster size. (make)
make a blow-up of

1 Students who decide to *drop out* may lose every opportunity of studying for a career. (be)

2 'Can you start to *wash up*, Fred, while I clear the table?' (do)

3 Publicity department needs to obtain further information *fed back* from Marketing before designing the advertisements. (get)

4 Jack's car *broke down* again on the way to work this morning. (have)

5 I've tried several times to take Peter out for a meal but he's always *brushed me off*. (give)

Exercise 57   noun forms of phrasal verbs

Explain the meaning of the *noun form* in *italics*.

Example
There has been so much trouble between the union and management that the workers are sure to organize *a walk-out* tomorrow.
a sudden strike

1 'News has just come in of another *hold-up* on the motorway – a lorry has tipped bricks onto the road.'

2 Several *outbreaks* of spontaneous applause proved the success of her speech to the farmworkers.

3 'Be sure to count the change correctly. We can't afford any more *slip-ups* in this department.'

4 John Elton was given a tremendous *write-up* when his latest album was released.

5 Regular *check-ups* with your dentist will prevent serious tooth decay.

Exercise 58   passive forms

Rewrite the sentences by putting the phrasal verbs (in *italics*) into the
passive form with *by*.

Example
Sally's boss *has asked her out*.
Sally *has been asked out by* her boss.

1 The facts *don't bear out* his story.
2 I'm very annoyed. I don't like people whom I hardly know *getting at*
   me.
3 The chairman *will hold* the matter *over* until the next meeting on May
   22nd.
4 Hardly anyone knew about the takeover. The management had
   hushed it *up* successfully.
5 *Is* anybody *attending to* that customer?

Exercise 59   opposites

Complete the sentences by choosing the idiom from the list which is
opposite in meaning to the idiom in *italics* in the exercise.

ring off	*come back*
take someone on	*turn something down*
take something down	*put something on*

Example
'I *put up* a notice yesterday reminding people to pay their club
membership fees.' – 'Did you? Well, it's not there now. Someone must
have _____ (it) _____ .'
taken it down

1 'If you're going to do some work on your car, you'd better *take off*
   those trousers and _____ these old jeans.'
2 I think Ben will accept the offer and *take on* the job, but Pete feels
   certain that he'll _____ (it) _____ .

3 'The doctor can't see any more patients at the moment, so if you don't want to wait it would be better to *go away* now and _____ again in an hour or so.'

4 They've *laid off* a hundred men at the chemical works, but they'll _____ (them) _____ again in a few months' time.

5 The New York office *called up* and I asked them to wait but when I picked up the phone a minute later the line was dead, so they must have _____ .

Exercise 60   position of the object

Complete the sentences by using the idiom given in brackets. Take care to position the object (also given in brackets) correctly.

Example
Gordon doesn't share his father's interest in technical things. In fact, he doesn't (take after) (him) in anything.
take after him

1 Janet didn't want to get involved in the scandal, but now the news has broken she says she'll never (live down) (it).

2 My father said that he wouldn't lend me the money, but if I (work on) (him) enough I'm sure he will.

3 'Nick looks tired and overworked. The stress and responsibility of the new job's beginning to (tell on) (him).'

4 'I need the names and addresses for all these invoice numbers. Could you (hunt up) (them) for me in the files, please?'

5 I expected Robertson to take the job, as I made him a good offer, but he (turn down) (it).

Exercise 61   position of the object

Complete the sentences by using the idiom given in brackets. Take care to position the object (also given in brackets) correctly.

Example
'I can't reach the salt. Would you mind (pass over) (it), please?'
passing it over

1 'I'm sorry that my application's rather late, but I need the visa at the end of May. Will you be able to (get through) (it) within a fortnight?'

2 'If you need the report urgently, I'll (get round) (it) to you this evening.'

3 I know what Dick's planning – I (see through) (him) a long time ago. He won't find it easy to trick me.

4 There wasn't much time to discuss the item concerning travel expenses, so we (pass over) (it) briefly. It will be raised at the next meeting.

5 'If you want that parcel to get to New Zealand in time for Christmas, you'd better (get off) (it) today!'

Exercise 62   position of the object

Substitute for each of the phrases in *italics* an idiom, chosen from the list, with the same meaning.

get through something	*see someone through*
get something through	*turn on someone*
see through someone	*turn someone on*

Example
I'd like the work to be finished as quickly as possible. Could you *complete it* by tomorrow lunchtime?
get through it

1 Patty's a great disco fan. She says the music really *excites her* and gets her dancing.

2 Paul imagined he could fool me but I had *noticed his deception* ages ago.

3 Our neighbour's dog shows its teeth every time it sees me. I'm sure it will *attack me* one day.

4 'I've reviewed your travel budget and I'll try my best to *have it approved* before the end of the week.'

5 'Of course I'll lend you some money! Will £25 be enough to *help you* until next week?'

3

Idioms, phrases and words from special areas of life

Exercise 63 banking

Complete the story by choosing the correct idiom from the list.

draw money out	*the bank rate*	*an open cheque*
a current account	*open an account*	*fill something in*
a deposit account	*dishonour a cheque*	*pay in*
a joint account	*a crossed cheque*	*bounce*

I must tell you about a customer who came into the bank this morning –
a strange old fellow, wearing a cap and a shabby raincoat. He said he
wanted to _____ with our bank. From his questions, it sounded as if he'd
never had a bank account before. So I explained to him that with a _____
you can _____ whenever you want, but that with a _____ you have to
give a week's notice. I told him that _____ is 12% at the moment.

  He seemed confused so I showed him a cheque book and explained
how to _____ – he'd obviously never seen one before! So I explained the
difference between a _____ and an _____ . And I asked him if he wanted
one signature on the cheque or whether it would be _____ together with
his wife. He said he didn't want his wife to know anything about it!
When I asked if there would be regular payments, he answered with a
grin, "Don't worry. My cheques won't _____ , if that's what you're
afraid of. The bank will never need to _____ that has my signature!"

  Then he said he'd like to open a deposit account immediately. When I
asked him how much he wanted to _____ , he brought out a parcel
wrapped in brown paper. He opened it and there were over 5000 pounds
tied up with string and rubber bands! I tried not to look surprised and he
said, "That's to start off with. What I put in tomorrow depends on how
much I win on the horses today!"

Exercise 64   buying and selling

Complete the conversation by choosing the correct idiom from the list.

use hire-purchase *set up shop*
pay cash *pay through the nose*
have goods on approval *sell like hot cakes*
shop around *put prices up*
buy in bulk *cut-price*
bring prices down

'Hallo. Are you shopping here nowadays? Haven't I seen you in Sharp's a couple of times?'
    'I'm just comparing prices.'
    'Oh, and so you should! It pays you to _____ , I always say. I used to go to Sharp's. I was their first customer when they _____ here four years ago. But I don't buy there much now. I'll give you a tip – this shop's cheaper. They even let you _____ , so you can decide at home whether or not to buy them. You can't do that at Sharp's. But you do have to _____ here, they don't let you _____ ; they like to be sure of getting their money. Can't blame them really, not when so much of their stock is _____ , and it really is cheap, compared with Sharp's. Mr Sharp does what he wants with his prices – he _____ regularly, never _____ ! At Sharp's I used to _____ but I've found out that it's much cheaper here. Mr Sharp's quite friendly but they say his wife's very peculiar.'
    'When I see something really cheap, I _____ . I have over 20 tins of coffee at home. Look at this vase. Pretty, isn't it? And there are those new potato peelers! I hear everybody's buying them, they're _____ . Just look at those queues at the cash registers! By the way, my name's Doreen Watson. What's yours?'
    'Mrs Sharp.'

Exercise 65   health, illness, death

Complete the conversation by choosing the correct idiom from the list.

take a turn for the better   *not feel oneself*
play havoc with one's health   *be laid up*
look washed out   *shake (an illness) off*
run a temperature   *pass away*
go down with (an illness)   *push up the daisies*

'Have you heard about poor Mr Sykes! He's ＿＿＿ . The funeral's
tomorrow. And he was only in his mid-fifties!'
    'Yes, sudden heart attack. Very sad affair. But Mr Sykes told me that
he'd been ＿＿＿ for years – overworking, missing meals and sleep,
smoking heavily. And he always ＿＿＿ , very pale and tired. You can't
go on like that for ever, can you? But tell me, how's your husband?'
    'Well, he's had a bad cold for a week now, and he doesn't seem able to
＿＿＿ . Three of his mates have ＿＿＿ flu. It's just the time of the year for
it, cold and damp. He's felt so hot and has obviously been ＿＿＿ for two
days now, so I called in the doctor this morning. I don't want him to
＿＿＿ over Christmas, do I! He doesn't want to stay at home in bed, but
I told him that he'll soon be ＿＿＿ like poor Mr Sykes, if he doesn't look
after himself properly!'
    'Yes, indeed. You can't be too careful. And my Rex's not ＿＿＿ at the
moment, either. He's been very quiet. He's off his food, although I've
tempted him with all the things he likes best. But I think he must have
＿＿＿ now, because he was shouting at the neighbour's cat again this
morning!'

Exercise 66   holidays and travel

Complete the conversation by choosing the correct idiom from the list.

go on holiday	*a five-star hotel*	*travel light*
a globe-trotter	*first class*	*live out of a suit-case*
a scheduled flight	*economy class*	*go on a cruise*
a chartered flight	*a boarding-pass*	*make a world-trip*

'Is this your first flight?'

'Good lord, no! I use planes as other people use buses. I'm what people call a _____ . You name the country, I've been there.'

'Oh, lucky you.'

'But I never go on one of those _____ – no thank you, too much waiting about in small airports. I only use _____ . And I always go _____ , I like comfort and that extra attention from the cabin crew. I don't mind paying more.'

'But we're in the _____ .'

'Yes, unfortunately there were no first-class seats left when my secretary made the reservation. Quite annoying. I find there's so little room here.'

'Business trip?'

'Yes, I never _____ by air. I prefer ships for relaxing. My wife and I usually _____ – Caribbean, South Pacific, you know. Two years ago we _____ , it lasted 3 months and we sailed every ocean – but I can't afford so much time for holidays every year, of course.'

'I don't think flying about on business would suit me, having to _____ , sleeping somewhere different every night.'

'I only stay at _____ , of course – it's luxury all the way for me. And I always _____ , as I haven't time to wait for luggage at airports – I put a clean shirt in my briefcase. I'm a very busy man, one important business meeting after the other.'

'Look, there's your _____ on the floor. It must have dropped out of your pocket. Flight number BA 706? To Kuwait? But this flight's going to Beirut!'

Exercise 67   holidays and travel

Complete the conversation by choosing the correct idiom from the list.

a guided tour	*stay the night*	*go camping*
a package holiday	*put up at a hotel*	*pitch the tent*
a holiday-maker	*a bed-and-breakfast*	*break camp*
a coach-party	*thumb a lift*	*sleep in the open*

'Sue, my feet ache. I can't carry this heavy rucksack any further. I
must've been crazy to let you persuade me to _____ .'

'It's the first day of our holiday and you're complaining already. Since
we got off the train we've only walked ten miles!'

'Well, that's far enough for today. There's a lorry coming behind us.
I'm going to _____ . I'll ask the driver if he knows a _____ where we can
_____ .'

'But we've got a tent to sleep in! We're on a walking tour, remember.
And I'm really looking forward to _____ under the stars tonight.'

'I wish we'd booked a _____ to Spain instead!'

'You know how I hate organized travel, Joe, especially _____ ,
rumbling along the road making me feel sick. Who wants to be shut up
in a bus with noisy _____ all day? Not me!'

'Or we could have gone on a _____ to Italy with Alison and Jeff. They
wanted to join the Arts Council group in Venice.'

'You know I don't like travelling with other people. I like being free to
do as I please.'

'Well, I hope this is free enough for you – not a house or a car in sight.
We're miles away from civilization. How I'd love to _____ and take a
hot bath.'

'We're not going to a hotel, Joe. Let's look for a nice spot near the
river to _____ . And when the tent's up, I'll prepare a good meal. You'll
like it so much that you'll be sorry to _____ tomorrow morning, just you
wait.'

'Lovely meal? Tinned beans, tinned corned beef, tinned peaches, and
tinned coffee with tinned milk. I hope you remembered to pack the tin-
opener.'

'Er . . . tin-opener? Well, er . . . '

Exercise 68   motoring

Complete the conversation by choosing the correct idiom from the list.

a no-claims bonus	*the rush-hour*
jam on the brakes	*run into*
pull in	*have an accident*
to back out	*a write-off*
be stuck in a traffic jam	*turn on the engine*

'Hello, darling! Have you had a good day in town? I've been lying in the garden all day enjoying the sunshine.'

'No, I haven't had a good day! I've _____ with the car.'

'Oh, dear! Are you OK?'

'Yes, I'm OK, but the car isn't. It's not a _____ , but the repairs will come to at least £500.'

'Well, the insurance will cover that – but we'll lose our _____ , of course. Anyway, what happened?'

'Well, you see, it was around 5 o'clock, the _____ was in full swing, cars and buses everywhere and I'd been stationary, _____ for half an hour – so I was feeling very fed up. Then I saw a baker's shop and realized that I'd forgotten to buy the bread. So I looked for somewhere to park, and I saw a space in front of an entrance to a yard. There was a 'No Parking – Keep Exit Clear' sign, but I didn't think it would matter just for a few minutes. So I _____ carefully and parked. I bought the bread, hopped back into the car, _____ and was _____ when suddenly a huge delivery van appeared behind me! I _____ , but he couldn't stop, so he _____ me, of course. He was annoyed and started the usual rubbish about women drivers.'

'So your poor little Mini's had quite a day!'

'Well – the thing is, dear – er – when I went into the garage this morning, I couldn't start *my* car – so I'm afraid it was your car I was driving . . . '

Exercise 69   motoring

Complete the conversation by choosing the correct idiom from the list.

run in (a car)	*the motorway*	*the boot*
in top (gear)	*a test-drive*	*the bonnet*
put one's foot down	*have a smash*	*a write-off*

'Good afternoon, sir. May I show you one of our latest models?'

'Yes. That Rolls-Royce over there. We don't see so many in Texas.'

'Oh, you're from America, sir. Yes, it's a beautiful car – one of our most expensive and exclusive models, with a very powerful engine. She purrs like a kitten when she's _____ .'

'I _____ in my car a few weeks ago – unfortunately it couldn't be repaired.'

'Oh, it was _____ , what bad luck!'

'May I have a look under the hood?'

'Oh, you mean _____ . That's what we call it here in England.'

'And how big is the trunk?'

'You mean _____ . I'm sure you'll find it quite spacious.'

'And what top speed can it do on the turnpike?'

'On _____ , when the road's clear and you _____ , it almost takes off! You can take it for a _____ , if you'd like to, sir. But may I ask you not to rev up the engine because the car's new and it hasn't been _____ yet.'

'Don't you worry, I won't. I only want to feel how it rides. Why don't you drive me back to my hotel. That would be quite sufficient.'

(10 minutes later)

'Well, thanks for the ride. You've won me 20 dollars! I bet my wife that I'd be brought home in a Rolls-Royce today.'

Exercise 70   telephoning

Complete the conversation by choosing the correct idiom from the list.

a phone-box   *a bad line*   *ring off*
get through   *a crossed line*   *take the call*
the line is engaged *go dead*   *the ringing tone*
out of order   *be cut off*   *hold the line*

'Hello! Tim! I've just been trying to ring my brother Nick at work, but
I've had a terrible job _____ to him. First of all, it took me half an hour
to find a _____ that worked – the first three I went into were all _____ . I
dialled Nick's number and heard _____ , then there was silence, nothing!
The line had simply _____ . I dialled again and got a wrong number – a
Mrs Winterbottom who was very annoyed at being disturbed. The third
time Nick must have been phoning someone himself, because _____ .
The fourth time I dialled, I got _____ ! I could hear two people having a
rather personal conversation. I was more successful the fifth time, I got
through to Nick's secretary. She asked me to _____ . I heard her tell Nick
that it was me – heard her asking him if he wanted to _____ . He
naturally said Yes, and we exchanged a few words, then for some reason
we _____ , and the connection was lost. By this time I was very angry. I
dialled a sixth time and I got Nick's secretary – at least, I suppose it was
her, because it was such a _____ that I could hardly hear what she was
saying above all the crackling and buzzing. So I had to _____ . Then I
tried again later and his secretary calmly told me that Nick had just left
his office for the afternoon and wouldn't be back!'

'Poor old you! But what was it that you wanted to tell your brother so
urgently?'

'That my home telephone's out of order! He's the head of the Fault
Section at the Post Office.'

Exercise 71   work and industrial relations

Complete the conversation by choosing the correct idiom from the list.

a white-collar worker	*on night-shift*	*a picket line*
work overtime	*a lock-out*	*a work-to-rule*
put in for a rise	*to black-leg*	*go on the dole*
come out on strike		

'Bill! I haven't seen you in this pub for a while. What'll it be? A pint of bitter?'

'Thanks, Mac. I've been _____ for the past six weeks, that's why you haven't seen me here in the evenings.'

'And I've been working all day Saturday and Sunday for the past three weeks, getting some extra money for the holidays.'

'The chance of _____ must be nice for you. I suppose you heard about the strike down at the car factory?'

'Not all the details.'

'Well, the union _____ of 20%. Since management refuse to negotiate, the union decided on _____, which slowed down production a lot. But when that didn't prove effective with the management, we all _____. Not all the men wanted to stop working, so some tried to _____, but the strikers organized _____, and that put an end to it. Of course, the _____ in their offices and the directors have every reason to be satisfied with their big salaries.'

'Now, be fair, Bill. They have their troubles, too. Anyway, how did the strike end?'

'Well, the management threatened us with _____ if we didn't accept 5% and since many of the men were afraid of losing their jobs and having to _____, we lowered our claim to 10%, and this was finally accepted. We're all reasonably satisfied now.'

4

Idioms using words for animals, colours, parts of the body, time

Exercise 72   animals

Complete the sentences by choosing the correct word from the list.

cat   donkey   goose   bee   dog   horse

Example
'Michael was hoping that Jean would spend the weekend fishing with him in Scotland – just the two of them, of course. Then her brother arrived unexpectedly, so they had to take him with them.' – 'Poor old Michael! That really *cooked his* _____ , didn't it!'
goose

1 My Uncle Bert lives on vegetables and nuts. He *has a* _____ *in his bonnet* about living to be a hundred and won't eat anything that contains animal fat.

2 'How did you find out? It was a secret!' – 'Marion told me.' – 'Oh, Marion. Well, she would *let the* _____ *out of the bag*. She couldn't keep her mouth shut if you paid her.'

3 The chief accountant took a lot of trouble to explain the firm's cash-flow problems but it still makes no sense at all. I'm afraid that trying to explain money matters to me is rather like *flogging a dead* _____ .

4 I agree that Tim's report is brilliant, but he must have got his assistant to *do the* _____ *work*, compiling all the facts and figures from miles of computer printout.

5 The roof's fallen in, the floors are rotting and the garden's run wild – what a pity to let such a lovely old house *go to the* _____ like that.

Exercise 73   animals

Complete the sentences by choosing the correct idiom.

Example
Michelle has this annoying habit of interrupting you in the middle of a
sentence. She never lets you finish what you want to say. It really _____ .
cook one's goose   get one's goat   make a beast of oneself
gets my goat

1 'I'd rather visit George tomorrow on the way back from Peter's. We
  could then _____ as it would save us having to make two separate
  journeys.'
  kill two birds with one stone   hold one's horses   flog a dead horse

2 'Oh dear – I'm beginning to get nervous now. I always _____ just
  before an exam starts, don't you?'
  have butterflies in one's stomach   go at a snail's pace   smell a rat

3 'How do you know that Ed is going to be posted to Madrid? Nobody
  else seems to know anything about it.' – 'Oh, I _____ , Ed's boss.'
  be top dog   take the bull by the horns   get it from the horse's mouth

4 Tim Spence didn't stop eating yesterday at the party. I've never seen a
  child of his age eat so much! He had cakes and biscuits in both hands
  all the time. He really _____ .
  be a fly in the ointment   make a pig of oneself   go at a snail's pace

5 Jim is really enjoying living out in the country. He says he _____ every
  day for a run before breakfast, and he's never felt better.
  have other fish to fry   get up with the lark   let sleeping dogs lie

Exercise 74   words related to animals

Explain the meanings of the idioms in *italics*.

Example
'We'll have to apply for a further grant of money for the research project. If I knew who *held the reins* on the grants committee, I'd write to him personally.'
was the most influential person

1 We've spent a lot of money on luxuries this year. We'll have to *draw in our horns* if we want to take that skiing holiday.

2 Our butcher seems to be a very rude, bad-tempered person, but in fact *his bark's worse than his bite* – and he sells the best meat in town.

3 'If that's a hint for me to lend you the money, then *you're barking up the wrong tree*. I've just had to borrow £100 from my bank.'

4 I don't like the idea of Jenny moving to the London office, but my brother lives there, too, and he says he'll *take her under his wing* until she makes friends and feels at home.

5 'Margie Robinson's worried about her teenage son. He races about wildly on his motorbike, disturbing all the neighbours, never paying any attention to what his parents say.' – 'Too much money and free time! They ought to limit his pocket-money. That would *clip his wings*!'

Exercise 75   colours

Complete the sentences by choosing the correct word from the list.

blue   white   yellow   black   green   grey

Example
We've a new shop assistant in our department, but she's rather _____
– a bit naïve and inexperienced. I don't think she'll sell much!
green

1 'I've paid off my overdraft at last – and its such a reassuring feeling to
   be back *in the* _____ again!'

2 'I got a telegram this morning telling me I'd won a lot of money on the
   football pools. I can hardly believe it! I hadn't checked my coupon, so
   it was completely *out of the* _____ .'

3 'I'm surprised at you! Fancy saying you had a dental appointment – I
   saw you queueing for the cinema.' – 'Well, it was only a little _____ *lie*
   so that I could leave the office early.'

4 We all wish George would behave more responsibly. His parents are
   so concerned about him – he's turned them both _____ with worry.

5 'Don't get upset about Thomas. He may threaten to send a note to the
   supervisor criticizing your work but he'll never do it. He has *a* _____
   streak in him and is much too afraid of being unpopular.'

Exercise 76   colours

Complete the sentences by choosing the correct idiom from the list.

a bolt from the blue   *red tape*
a red herring   *a white lie*
the black sheep   *in someone's black books*

Example
'Were you really ill in bed on the night of Wendy's party, or did you tell
her _____ , so as not to hurt her feelings?' – 'Yes, I did – just a little one.'
a white lie

1 'What did you think of the Prime Minister's speech?' – 'Too many
   _____ . There are so many important issues which concern the nation,
   and most of them weren't mentioned at all.'

2 It's time the government made it easier to get work permits. I'm sure
   all the _____ puts off many foreigners with valuable skills from
   coming to live and work here.

3 Tina came home one weekend and told her parents that she had got
   engaged to Phil. It was _____ for them, because they didn't even know
   that he was her steady boyfriend.

4 'If you see Michael, don't mention me. I'm afraid I was very rude to
   him last night, so now I'm really _____ .'

5 'Matthew and Winston are both highly respectable lawyers. But the
   youngest son, Simon, went off to Australia after a wild affair with a
   strip-club dancer.' – 'Ah, so Simon's the _____ , is he?'

Exercise 77   colours

Explain the meanings of the idioms in *italics*.

Example
'I've worked on this project for months never knowing if the Board would accept my designs. Now I've *been given the green light* and, best of all, a realistic budget.'
been allowed to go ahead with it

1 'I planted some shrubs and small trees in my garden a month ago, but it doesn't look as if they're going to grow.' – 'Why don't you ask Ted what to do about them? He's *got green fingers.*'

2 I'll never forget the day when the results of our final exams came out. Nine or ten of us got together and celebrated until late into the night. We really *painted the town red.*

3 'Last night I passed Barry in the car park. He was obviously *in a brown study* because I spoke to him, but he didn't answer – I don't think he knew I was there.'

4 'I haven't forgotten that today's *a red letter day*, darling. I've already put some champagne in the fridge.'

5 I wish your Uncle Charles hadn't given us that six-foot-high statue as a wedding present. It may be a beautiful museum piece, but in a two-roomed flat I'm afraid it's a bit of *a white elephant.*

Exercise 78   parts of the body

Complete the sentences by choosing the correct idiom.

Example
'Didn't Jim tell his wife that he'd decided to sell the car?' – 'No, and that's what their big quarrel was about. He did it _____ .'
up to one's neck   by the skin of one's teeth   behind someone's back
behind her back

1 'Would you believe it! The day after Dave resigned he was telephoned from Tokyo and offered a post there at twice his salary!' – 'Typical! Trust Dave to _____ yet again.'
fall on one's feet   keep one's hand in   stick one's neck out

2 We've got a new secretary, fresh from the secretarial college. She's a little naïve, still _____ .
wet behind the ears   on one's toes   a pain in the neck

3 'I've decided to tell the boss that it was my mistake. He'll find out himself eventually, so I may as well _____ now.'
lose face   pick someone's brains   make a clean breast of it

4 Maureen thinks one of the clerks is attracted to her, but she doesn't want to encourage him so she's _____ .
be within elbow reach   not turn a hair   keep someone at arm's length

5 'Have you found those files yet?' – 'No, I can't remember where I left them and I've been _____ for hours.'
fight tooth and nail   rack one's brains   go off one's head

Exercise 79   parts of the body

Substitute for each of the phrases in *italics* an idiom, chosen from the list, with the same meaning.

keep one's hair on	*put one's back into it*
lose face	*keep one's hand in*
keep one's fingers crossed	*see eye to eye*

Example
I'm afraid my husband and I *are not of the same opinion* on the matter.
do not see eye to eye

1 'I'm taking my driving test tomorrow, so *wish me luck*.'
2 'OK, OK! *Don't get angry*! I won't do it again!'
3 If you'd like Bob to repair your car for you, I'm sure he'd be glad to do it. He used to work as a car mechanic, and he likes to *practise at it*.
4 If you really don't want to *be humiliated* in the office, you should say you accept the reasons for losing promotion and show your determination to improve.
5 'Your team is not getting on very well with the Philips order, are they? If you want to deliver the stock by Friday, they'll really have to *work their hardest*.'

Exercise 80   time

Substitute for each of the phrases in *italics* an idiom, chosen from the list, with the same meaning.

bide one's time	*for the time being*
do time	*in the nick of time*
take one's time over something	*time after time*

Example
'I'd like you to make a really good job of writing the report, so *do it slowly and carefully*.'
take your time over it

1 I arrived late at the station and almost missed my train. I just managed to jump on it *at the very last moment.*

2 I've told Jones *repeatedly* not to be late for work but he doesn't seem to care.

3 I don't think Jack has serious intentions of staying in his present job. I suspect he's just *waiting for a better opportunity to come along.*

4 'What's Janice doing these days?' – 'Well, she's starting college in October, so *at present* she's helping her father in the shop.'

5 'I wonder if Jerry McGregor had anything to do with the supermarket robbery?' – 'No, he couldn't have. You forget – he's still *in prison* at the moment.'

Exercise 81   time

Complete the sentences by choosing the correct idiom.

Example
'Surely that clock can't be right.' – 'No, its very unreliable. It's been _____ for the last few days. I'll have to get it repaired.'
keep good time   keep wasting time   keep bad time
keeping bad time

1 'I'm sorry I can't stop for a chat but I _____ at the moment. Can I ring you this evening?'
be behind the times   be pressed for time   be in good time

2 'Get on with your work and stop gossiping! You're _____ again.'
wasting time   doing time   killing time

3 'Sorry I'm late. Am I still _____ for some coffee or has the meeting started?'
in time   on time   at times

4 If you can't mend the tap, ask John to do it. He's so good and quick at repairing things – he'll do it _____ .
in the nick of time   in time   in no time

5 'It's December already – soon be Christmas.' – 'That's true. It's amazing how quickly this year's gone – _____ !'
in times gone by   time's up   time flies

Exercise 82   time

Complete the conversation by choosing the correct idiom from the list.

a nightcap	*keep regular hours*
work nights	*be getting on in years*
a night-owl	*the morning after the night before*
at any moment	*once in a blue moon*
an unearthly hour	

'Morning, Paul! You look rather tired – or is it a hangover?'

'No! It' not _____ , if that's what you mean. I hardly ever have too much to drink now, only _____ such as on an important anniversary. And it's early to bed for me these days, too. I used to be a _____ when I was a student, but I _____ now that I've got a job. But I'm tired this morning because I was with some friends last night – a film and a meal – and when I got back to my room, I wasn't feeling like sleep. So I had a large whisky as _____ , and got into bed. I must have fallen asleep, because the next thing I knew my landlady was shaking me, saying she was sorry to wake me up at such _____ , but she'd heard noises in the kitchen and thought maybe a burglar had broken in – and would I have a look.'

'But where was her husband?'

'He's a shift-worker and this week he _____ , so I was the only other person in the house. Mrs Pearson's _____ and is a bit nervous, so I told her to go back to bed and that I'd take a look.'

'And did you?'

'Yes. I crept down the stairs, armed with a tennis racket.'

'And then?'

'I saw a dark figure in the kitchen with a knife in his hand. I expected him to look up _____ so I was just about to hit him with the racket when he shouted out, "Hey, it's me!" It was Mr Pearson. He'd forgotten his sandwiches!'

5
Idioms using adjectives and nouns

Exercise 83   dead

Complete the sentences by choosing the correct idiom from the list.

be dead against something   *a dead end*
be dead right   *come to a dead end*
go dead   *cut someone dead*

Example
You said that I'd be sorry I bought Andrew's old car, and you _____ ,
I am! I've already paid out a fortune in repairs.'
were dead right

1 I don't think the strike will be settled for weeks yet. The negotiations
   seem to have _____ .
2 'I don't know what's the matter with Mary, but for some reason she
   doesn't want to speak to me. When I passed her in the street this
   morning, she just _____ .'
3 'I had difficulty in finding the way. I took a wrong road and it turned
   out to be _____ , so I had to turn round and go back.'
4 I think the phone's out of order. When I tried to ring Paul the line
   simply _____ .
5 'Have you been able to persuade your wife about the camping trip?' –
   'I'm afraid not. She _____ the idea.'

Exercise 84 **flat**

Substitute for each of the phrases in *italics* an idiom, chosen from the list, with the same meaning.

fall flat	*go flat out*	*be flat broke*
go flat	*that's flat*	*be in a flat spin*

Example
We didn't stay long at Jack's place last night. After dinner the conversation *became uninteresting*, so we decided to leave.
went flat

1 'Could you lend me five pounds for the weekend? I'm afraid *I've no money at all.*'
2 'How did you manage to get here so early?' – 'Luckily, there was very little traffic on the motorway, so I *went as fast as I could* all the way.'
3 My brother was so embarrassed when he gave the toast that no one heard any of his jokes and so they *made no impression at all.*
4 I'm afraid I caught John at a bad time. He was *in a state of confusion,* trying to clean the house, feed his children and listen to me, all at the same time.
5 'I won't have your Uncle Fred to stay. His feet smell, he eats enough for two and he watches television all night. Don't ask me again – I've said no and *it's my final word.*'

Exercise 85 **good**

Explain the meanings of the idioms in *italics*.

Example
'Has the baby behaved himself while I've been out, Sheila?' – 'He's been *as good as gold* all day.'
very well-behaved

1 'Dick Reynolds is back from America.' – 'What! When he left he swore to me that he was leaving this country *for good*.'

2 '*It's a good job* I didn't go out this afternoon as I'd planned to. The plumber came unexpectedly to mend the leak.'

3 'Didn't Carol say she would do your work for you on Friday, so that you could take the day off? You'd better ask if her offer still *holds good*.'

4 I've applied for a job in your department, so I hope you'll *put in a good word for me* with your manager when the applications are considered.

5 I went out dancing *a good deal* when I was living in London.

Exercise 86   hard

Complete the sentences by choosing the correct idiom from the list.

be hard pressed   *be hard up*   *take a hard line*
be hard hit   *be as hard as nails*   *a hard and fast rule*

Example
George asked for paternity leave in order to help with the children while his wife was in hospital with the new baby. However, his boss _____ .
He refused even one day off.
was as hard as nails

1 I'd like to buy a new winter coat, but I can't afford one. I _____ at the moment.

2 The management is determined not to give in to the strikers. They obviously believe that the only way to deal with the union is to _____ .

3 'Can you give me _____ for the use of the Present Perfect in English?' – 'Sorry, I can't – there isn't one.'

4 Motorists have _____ by the sudden and unexpected rise in the price of petrol.

5 'I shall _____ to get the report finished by tomorrow, but I'll try my best.'

Exercise 87   high

Substitute for each of the phrases in *italics* an idiom, chosen from the list, with the same meaning.

be in high spirits   *high and low*
be for the high jump   *the high life*
get on one's high horse   *high and dry*

Example
The new job gives me a company car, a place in the director's dining-room and a chance to travel all over the world. I'm not used to *luxurious living* but I intend to enjoy myself!
the high life

1 I bought some new shoes a week ago and now I can't find them. I've looked *everywhere* for them.
2 I think Rachel must have received some good news – she's *been in a very cheerful mood* all day.
3 'When the boss discovers that you've fiddled your expense account you'll *be due for severe punishment.* I'd resign immediately, if I were you.'
4 David could be quite a nice person to work with, if only he didn't *become so proud and haughty* every time someone criticizes him.
5 If I hadn't found a taxi, I'd have been left *stranded.* I'd missed both the last bus and the last train.

Exercise 88   poor

Explain the meanings of the idioms in *italics*.

Example
'It doesn't seem worth while to spend so much time in the vegetable garden. You have such *poor soil* – nothing seems to grow well.'
soil that will not produce healthy plants

1 'Carol *has been in* such *poor health* lately. Could it be due to overwork?'

2 'Well, Stephen may think he has something useful to contribute to the discussion but everyone *has* such *a poor opinion of* him that no one will listen.'

3 Jobs at the car plant *are in poor supply* since the huge increases in the price of petrol affected the number of cars sold in Europe.

4 'I'm sorry I'm late. My alarm-clock didn't work this morning.' – 'That's *a poor excuse* if ever I heard one.'

5 'You'll have to repaint these windows completely. The foreman will never pass such *poor work*.'

Exercise 89   **short**

Complete the sentences by choosing the correct idiom.

Example
'I'm afraid I've _____ coffee. Would you like tea instead?'
short measure   run short of   go short of
run short of

1 'Before you leave the shop, I warn you – count your money. The new assistant has given me _____ three times already this week.'
short shrift   short measure   short change

2 I'm surprised to see that you _____ the report I asked you to write. I thought it would take you much longer.
fall short of   go short of   make short work of

3 All the men at the car factory are _____ . Jack's only been at work three days this week. Apparently there are no orders coming in.
in short supply   taken short   on short time

4 I was christened Elizabeth, but most people call me Beth _____ .
in short   for short   short for

5 'How did you enjoy the new film version of "Gone with the Wind"? – 'Not very much, I'm afraid. It _____ our expectations, after all the talk about it and the good write-up in the press.'
be short of   stop short of   fall short of

Exercise 90   **thick   thin**

Complete the sentences by choosing the correct idiom from the list.

vanish into thin air   *as thick as thieves*
in thick with someone   *thin on top*
lay it on thick   *a bit thick*

Example
'Donald's getting rather _____ , isn't he?' – 'Yes, he'll be bald by the time
he's 40.'
thin on top

1 'Mrs Nelson told me how she nearly died last year.' – 'Oh, you
   mustn't believe everything she tells you. When she talks about her
   aches and pains she always _____ .'

2 'I didn't realize that Jane and Anne were such good friends.' – 'Oh,
   yes. They've been _____ ever since they started doing business
   together five years ago.'

3 Be sure not to mention this to Tom. He's _____ the branch secretary,
   and he'd certainly tell him anything you said. That could be disastrous
   for you.

4 I can't find my watch. I've looked everywhere for it. It just seems to
   have _____ .

5 'You spent Friday evening in the gymnasium, most of Saturday at a
   football match and now you ask me to save you Sunday lunch while
   you play squash with Harry! It's _____ !'

Exercise 91 **end**

Substitute for each of the phrases in *italics* an idiom, chosen from the list, with the same meaning.

in the end	*be at a loose end*
make both ends meet	*go off the deep end*
odds and ends	*get hold of the wrong end of the stick*

Example
I had to stay in Milan overnight because the last flight to Paris was fully booked. I *had nothing special to do* so I rang Camilla and asked her out to dinner.
was at a loose end

1 I tried to explain to Pete how I came to have the accident, but when he saw the damage I'd done to his car, he *suddenly became angry* and started shouting at me.

2 Jane asked Bill if he had time to drive her home, but *he mistook her intention* and asked her over to his flat!

3 The committee seemed determined to cut our production budget but Angela made a superb defence of the various projects and we won *finally*.

4 'I'll be home later than usual this evening – I've got a lot of *small matters* to attend to at the office.'

5 With higher taxes, lower profit margins and reduced export opportunities, it's become increasingly difficult to *stay out of debt*.

Exercise 92   **line**

Substitute for each of the phrases in *italics* an idiom, chosen from the list, with the same meaning.

drop someone a line   shoot a line
along the right lines   take the line of least resistance
all along the line   toe the line

Example
'Don't forget to *write to us* when you have time!'
drop us a line

1 I wouldn't take what Julian says very seriously if I were you. Most of what he says is just *lying and exaggerating*.
2 It's a difficult problem to solve, but I think I'm working *in the right direction*.
3 'Has Max decided how best to get out of his dilemma yet?' – 'No, but if I know Max, he'll *find the easiest way of doing it.*'
4 The referee warned Davis twice that if he didn't *obey the rules* he would be sent off the field.
5 'Don't you agree that the severe drop in profits proves that we adopted the wrong advertising policy?' – 'Yes, it's clear that we made mistakes *at every stage* in that area.'

Exercise 93   **mind**

Explain the meanings of the idioms in *italics*.

Example
Jenny said she'd lend me a book on Chinese music, but she hasn't brought it with her. *It must have slipped her mind.*
She must have forgotten about it.

1 '*I've a good mind* to take this pullover back to the shop and complain. When I washed it, the colour came out.'

2 If I were you, I wouldn't let your father-in-law interfere so much. It's time *you spoke your mind* and told him that you can run your house yourself.

3 'There is a schizophrenia discussion group in the university and *I've half a mind* to join.'

4 'What's wrong with Maureen? She seems a bit gloomy.' – '*She's got something on her mind* – probably another quarrel with her boyfriend.'

5 *I'm in two minds* whether to accept the job in New Zealand or go to Brussels where I'll earn more money.

Exercise 94   point

Complete the sentences by choosing the correct idiom.

Example
In my opinion, Carol's much too young to get married. But what I think is _____ . She'll never listen to what I've got to say.
a case in point   beside the point   in point of fact
beside the point

1 'Come on, Brian, I know you never lend things, but _____ and let me borrow your guitar. I promise that I'll take good care of it.'
stretch a point   come to the point   miss the point

2 'Don't waste time so much! _____ and let's get on with the rest of the business.'
wander off the point   take someone's point   get to the point

3 'I'm afraid I can't _____ writing a six-page letter when you could settle the matter in two minutes on the telephone.'
see the point of   make a point of   be no point in

4 I suppose I could write a long letter of complaint to the manufacturers, but then, _____ ? They won't give me a new washing machine!
what's more to the point   what's the point   if it comes to the point

5 John probably told you that he had no trouble getting into university, but _____ he had four refusals before he finally got given a place.
get to the point   a pointed remark   in point of fact

Exercise 95   **way**

Substitute for each of the phrases in *italics* an idiom, chosen from the list, with the same meaning.

go out of one's way   mend one's ways   have it both ways
on the way out   out of the way   have one's own way

Example
Steve does nothing but enjoy himself – he hardly ever does any work. If he doesn't *improve his behaviour*, he'll lose his chance of promotion.
mend his ways

1 The trouble is you want plenty of free time and a successful career. You can't *have two contradictory things*. Either get a decent job or be a drop-out.

2 Tim likes his new job, but it's on the other side of town and rather *difficult to reach*.

3 Mary's got a very strong personality. She always manages to *get what she wants*.

4 One of my favourite pop groups is 'Poison', but they seem to be *losing popularity* now. You don't hear their records much these days.

5 Don and Sally *did everything possible* to help me when my wife was in hospital.

Exercise 96   **word**

Complete the sentences by choosing the correct idiom.

Example
Although it was the van-driver's fault, he told the police that I had
caused the accident. Because there were no witnesses, it's _____ , I'm
afraid.
his word against mine   a man of his word   a play on words
his word against mine

1 It's no use trying to tell Nigel anything important – whenever I'm with
  him he chatters so much I can hardly _____ .
  be word perfect   get a word in edgeways   give someone one's word

2 It's no use translating English idioms _____ . They never make sense!
  word for word   in a word   by word of mouth

3 'Bill's been neglecting his work lately. I'll _____ with his supervisor
  and find out if anything is bothering him.'
  put in a good word   mark my words   have a word

4 Brian swears that he didn't do the damage – and since I can't prove it,
  I'll have to _____ .
  have the last word   take someone's word for it   eat one's words

5 'Lucy said that she'd babysit for us on Saturday evening, so as long as
  she _____ , we'll be able to go to the concert after all.'
  keep one's word   go back on one's word   coin a word

Exercise 97   **world**

Explain the meanings of the idioms in *italics*.

Example
To judge from the way Brian talks about his new girlfriend, she must be really *out of this world.*
magnificent

1 Mick's father has offered to buy him a new guitar, but he's got so attached to his old one that he wouldn't part with it *for the world.*

2 'Isn't that girl in the red trousers Karen?' – 'No, it can't be her, she's on holiday at the moment. But I must admit that she's *for all the world like* Karen.'

3 'But I don't want to *get on in the world*, Dad. I'm much happier living with Charles and sharing his pottery kiln.'

4 Why has Miss Evans *come down in the world* so much lately? She used to run her own little business, but now she's working as a shop assistant.

5 Dick doesn't live with his wife any more, but his three sons still *mean the world* to him.

Exercise 98   pairs of adjectives

Complete the sentences by choosing the correct idiom.

Example
'Where can I have put my car keys? I've been looking for them _____ all morning!'
fair and square   right and left   high and low
high and low

1 Martin would get on much better with everybody if only he didn't have such a _____ manner. He always gives the impression of wanting to appear superior.
   rich and poor   great and small   high and mighty

2 I'm afraid I wasn't consulted about the arrangements. When I found out about them they were already _____ so there was nothing I could do.
   cut and dried   black and blue   for good or ill

3 I warn you – don't let Harry repair your record-player. He does everything in such a _____ way that it'll break down again in no time.
   meek and mild   right and wrong   rough and ready

4 'Don't bother to write a long speech – a few words will be enough. Make it _____ .'
   short and sweet   cut and dried   more or less

5 'Can I rely on your support at the meeting? I don't want to be left _____ when I put forward my proposal.'
   free and easy   high and dry   slow but sure

Exercise 99   pairs of nouns

Complete the sentences by choosing the correct idiom from the list.

life and soul   *skin and bone*   *heaven and earth*
body and soul   *for love or money*   *wear and tear*

Example
Jack has no intention of becoming a policeman. In fact, he says that with the increase in mob violence in the cities he wouldn't take on such a job _____ .

for love or money

1 'I can't have the contract ready for signature this evening but I'll move _____ to complete it by the end of the week.'
2 Jim was in such a good mood at Anne's house and told such funny stories about his trip to Paris. Everyone agreed he was the _____ of the party.
3 Our furniture used to look very nice but with the constant _____ of four children, it's now very shabby indeed.
4 'Then he knelt down and said "I'm yours _____ " and I burst out laughing.'
5 'Have you seen Mr Jones since he returned to work after his operation? He's so thin, just _____ .'

Exercise 100

Complete the conversation by choosing the correct idiom from the list.

a blind date	*a hard drinker*	*a soft spot*
a chance meeting	*second thoughts*	*a stag-party*
a confirmed bachelor	*seventh heaven*	*cold feet*
Dutch courage		

'Hi, Richard! I'm just on my way to Pete O'Connor's place. He's asked a few friends over this evening.'

'Isn't your wife going with you?'

'No, not tonight, it's strictly for men only – it's _____ . Pete's getting married tomorrow.'

'Pete's getting married? That is a surprise! I thought he'd lost interest since that affair with the French girl. He told me himself that he'd become _____ and would never marry.'

'Yes, that was a sad story. They were engaged to be married. Then she went off with another man. That upset Pete a lot. In fact, he became rather _____ after that, always in pubs and clubs.'

'Well, Pete always did like a good drink. Who's he marrying?'

'A red-head called Pat.'

'A red-head, eh? Pete always had _____ for red-heads. How did he meet her? Did his brother arrange _____ for him with yet another girl from his office?'

'No, nothing like that this time. It was purely _____ , at a disco, I think. I've never seen him so happy. He's in _____ , I can tell you!'

'That's good news. I hope he's made the right decision and won't have _____ about it tomorrow!'

'I doubt it. He's old enough to know what he's doing. But I remember getting _____ myself on the night before my wedding. My father comforted me with a bottle of brandy – said it would give me _____ . That was over ten years ago.'

'And how much brandy have you needed since then?'

Exercise 101

Complete the sentences by choosing the correct idiom.

Example
'If you see Ian don't mention the cricket team. He expected to be made
captain but he wasn't.' – 'Oh, I see. It's ____ with him, is it?'
a raw deal   a hot potato   a sore point
a sore point

1 'Do you think we'll be able to persuade Jones to extend the contract?'
   – 'Well, I expect he'll make trouble when he hears that we can't keep
   to the agreed delivery date. He's ____ to deal with.'
   a big shot   a stuffed shirt   a tough customer

2 'Did Simon pass his exam?' – 'Yes, but only just. It was ____ . The
   pass mark was 45% and he got 46%.'
   a ticklish situation   a tight spot   a close thing

3 'Wow! That was ____ ! I almost hit that cyclist. The traffic lights
   must have been at red and I didn't even see them!'
   a security risk   a near thing   fast living

4 'So Morrison is managing director of the company? That's news to
   me. I didn't realize that he was such ____ .'
   a big top   a marked man   a big shot

5 'We can't all get in the car. There isn't enough room for six people and
   a dog.' – 'Well, we can try, can't we? Although I do admit that it'll be
   rather ____ .'
   a close shave   a narrow escape   a tight squeeze

Exercise 102

Complete the sentences by adding the correct word, chosen from the list, to the noun in *italics*.

open   inside   rolling   flying   plain   cat

Example
The thief entered the house by a small attic window. Goodness knows how he got up there. He was obviously a professional ____ *burglar*.
cat burglar

1 'Don't bother to make tea for us. We can't stay long – we're just on *a
____ visit*.'
2 'Where's Pete these days? The last time I heard from him he was in
Paris, before that he was in Cairo, and he was talking about getting a
job in Tokyo. He never stays in one place very long. He's *a ____
stone* if ever there was one.'
3 'I didn't know that John was so friendly with his head of department.'
– 'Oh yes. Everybody knows – but nobody speaks about it. It's been
an ____ secret for months.'
4 'How's Jack getting on with his new business?' – 'Well, it was all
____ sailing at first, no difficulties at all. But he's had a few problems
recently – you know, inflation, strong pound, the bank rate ...'
5 'Have the police found out who did the supermarket break-in?' – 'No,
not yet, but they're fairly sure it was *an ____ job*, so they're
questioning all the staff very thoroughly.'

Exercise 103

Complete the conversation by choosing the correct idiom from the list.

a bed of roses   *the pros and cons*   *a fish out of water*
a cog in the machine   *the tricks of the trade*   *the gift of the gab*
the crack of dawn   *ups and downs*   *the ins and outs*
the lion's share   *not trust someone an inch*

'Have you heard about Sam? He wants to start up a business of his own, selling fruit and vegetables.'

'Really? Whatever gave him that idea?'

'Well, apparently he's fed up of being one of a thousand wage-earners at the firm, just _____ . He wants to make some real money before it's too late. And he's taking Jerry Dobson into partnership with him.'

'Oh, well, Jerry's the right sort of man to get a business going. He's a good talker.'

'Yes, I agree. Jerry's certainly got _____ . And it won't take him long to learn _____ . He used to have a small grocery store years ago, so he'll know _____ of running such a business already. But Sam'll have to watch out that Jerry doesn't take _____ of the profits!'

'Right. I would _____ myself.'

'Well, I've warned Sam that it won't be _____ at first, and he'll have his _____ with the business. He'll have to get up every morning at _____ to fetch the produce from the market, and in that world he'll feel like _____ until he gets used to it. But he says he's weighed up _____ carefully and he thinks he can make a success of it.'

Exercise 104

Complete the sentences by choosing the correct idiom.

Example
'Everybody's saying that Charles is going to marry Diana. It's only a
rumour but it's certainly _____ .'
a leap in the dark   a port in any storm   the talk of the town
the talk of the town

1 'People always say that money is _____ , yet everyone is anxious to
   have lots of it!'
   the fall of man   the root of all evil   a pillar of society
2 Rachel is always day-dreaming, building _____ . It's time she came
   down to earth and found herself a proper job.
   a bed of roses   castles in the air   a tower of strength
3 They say that every family has _____ , but if this affair comes to light,
   it'll certainly be the ruin of Lord Featherbed.
   an apple of discord   a skeleton in the cupboard   a snake in the grass
4 'Joe was depending on that £10,000 loan from the bank. He's already
   signed the contract for the new house. Now he learns that the bank
   won't lend him more than £2,000.' – 'That's _____ for him, isn't it?'
   a smack in the eye   a slap in the face   a fly in the ointment
5 I told you that after a week or so nobody would even mention the
   affair – and I was right. It was all a lot of talk and excitement about
   nothing, just _____ .
   a storm in a tea-cup   a flash in the pan   a leap in the dark

6

Idioms using prepositions and adverbs

Exercise 105

Complete the sentences by using the noun given in brackets with the correct prepositions.

Example
'I'm not _____ (the habit) _____ smoking strong cigars, but if you offered me one now, I'd take it.'
in the habit of

1 'I've been asked to give a vote of thanks _____ (behalf) _____ all our club members.'
2 These new machines produce glass bottles _____ (the rate) _____ two thousand per hour.
3 _____ (response) _____ the television appeal, thousands of viewers donated money in aid of the Flood Relief Fund.
4 'Look at these beautiful Japanese stamps. Roger gave me them _____ (exchange) _____ two sets of 1968 British special issue.
5 During my studies at university, I made friends with a large number of foreign students. I'm still _____ (contact) _____ many of them.

Exercise 106

Complete the sentences by choosing the correct idiom.

Example
_____ your insurance claim, would you please contact our branch office as soon as possible?
with regard to   out of regard for   in this regard
With regard to

1 I was just _____ ringing up to complain that my taxi hadn't arrived, when I heard it draw up outside.
at the point of   on the point of   at this point

2 _____ all the extra work at the office, I've decided to postpone my holidays.
in view of   with a view to   with the view of

3 Mrs Fairbanks is badly _____ a cleaning help. She can't manage that big house by herself any longer.
for want of   from want of   in want of

4 'Are you _____ valid travel documents – passport, entry visa and certificate of vaccination?'
in possession of   in the possession of   in possession

5 'I don't mind having Stevens on the Advisory Board, but I'm not _____ making him Chairman.'
in favour with   in favour of   out of favour

Exercise 107

Complete the sentences by choosing the correct idiom.

Example
'I'm sorry to disturb you but there's a man here in reception who won't
believe that you are busy and insists upon seeing you _____ .'
here and there   here, there and everywhere   here and now
here and now

1 'Have you ever been to Glasgow?' – 'Yes, but only _____ . I'm not
   very fond of the place.'
   on and off   once or twice   now and then

2 When Grandad starts talking about his adventures at sea, he doesn't
   know when to stop. He goes _____ for hours!
   again and again   over and over   on and on

3 The weather's very unsettled for April. It's even been snowing _____ .
   on and on   on and off   now and then

4 'How's Garry's broken leg coming along?' – 'Oh, it's much better,
   thanks. He's _____ now.'
   up and up   up and down   up and about

5 'The business is going quite well. We had our troubles at first, but
   _____ we can't complain.'
   by and large   by and by   by the by

7
Comparisons

Exercise 108

Complete the sentences by choosing a suitable comment. Use a comparison (as ... as ...) containing an adjective and a noun chosen from the lists.

adjectives
quick   warm   pale   fit   tough   deaf

nouns
ghost · leather   toast   fiddle   post   lightning

Example
'Anne invited me over for a meal last night, but it was a bit of a disaster. It took me so long to cut my steak and even longer to chew it – it was _____ .'

as tough as leather

1 'My father's well over seventy but he's incredibly healthy. He says he wants to join the London marathon – he's _____ .'
2 'Quickly! Find a chair for this patient, nurse. He's _____ and I think he's going to faint.'
3 'If you want Grandad to hear you, you'll have to shout louder than that – he's _____ .'
4 Phil has a marvellous head for figures. We were working on some invoices together. I was using a calculator but he's _____ and knew the answers before I did!
5 'I'm _____ in these new boots. Look how thick the fur lining is.'

Exercise 109

Complete the sentences by choosing the correct noun from the list.

sheet   grave   gold   brass   hills   bell

Example
I tried to get Jenkins to explain why he had resigned but he refused to say a word – *as silent as* _____ , in fact.
as silent as the grave

1 I spoke to Matthew on the phone this morning – a direct line from London to Tokyo. His voice was *as clear as* _____ .
2 'Has Kate been a good girl while I've been out?' – 'Yes, she has. She's been *as good as* _____ all day.'
3 'I didn't think that Mark would dare to ask you for help after the way he's treated you.' – 'Oh, you obviously don't know Mark. He's *as bold as* _____ .'
4 Luke must have got some bad news over the phone. When he put the receiver down, he just stared at us. He'd turned *as white as* _____ .
5 'Have you heard the news about Kevin's trip to Munich?' – 'Oh, you mean when he broke his leg on the airport escalator? That story's *as old as* _____ .'

Exercise 110

Complete the sentences by choosing the correct comparison containing the verb given in brackets and a noun chosen from the list.

glove   log   horse   bird   chimney   fish

Example
'After an eight-hour trek across the mountains, I bathed my feet, crept into my sleeping-bag, and (sleep) _____ .'
slept like a log

1 'I've never seen anyone eat like Tricia. I don't know where she puts so much food!' – 'You're right. She (eat) _____ .'

2 'I don't think I've ever seen Robin without a cigarette in his hand.' – 'No, neither have I. He (smoke) _____ .'

3 'Hello Tim! I hear you're breaking all the speed limits with your new sportscar.' – 'Yes, I am. She's a beauty. She (go) _____ .'

4 'I saw Jim Spence in the pub last night. He was putting down pints of bitter as if they were glasses of water.' – 'Oh yes, didn't you realize, he (drink) _____ ?'

5 'I think I'll buy these jeans. They don't even need any alterations, do they?' – 'No, they're perfect. They (fit) _____ .'

Exercise 111

Complete the sentences by choosing the correct comparison containing the noun given in brackets and a noun chosen from the list.

rhinoceros   ferret   water   sieve   bull   elephant

Example
'Did you remember to bring my gloves back?' – 'I'm sorry but I completely forgot! I've (memory) _____ .'
a memory like a sieve

1 Hilary isn't very happy in her new job but I expect she'll get used to it. Everything is so new to her that she feels like (fish) _____ .

2 I voted in favour of the new project at the meeting then Jackson reminded me that I argued strongly against it nine years ago. He never forgets anything. He has (memory) _____ .

3 'Sarah was so angry when I mentioned Frank's promotion. I didn't realize that she expected to get it herself.' – 'Yes, she's furious if the subject is mentioned. It's (red rag) _____ .'

4 I told Ken to his face that I didn't like his painting but he seemed completely insensitive to criticism. He has (hide) _____ .

5 'Neville says he wouldn't trust Bill with anything. He seems to have taken an instant dislike to him.' – 'Yes, he thinks Bill has (eyes) _____ and looks incapable of being kind.'

8
Proverbs

Exercise 112

Complete the sentences by choosing a suitable proverb from the list.

honesty is the best policy
absence makes the heart grow fonder
one's bark is worse than one's bite

beauty is only skin deep
better late than never
first come, first served

Example
'The sales start tomorrow and there's a fur coat in Harper's window that's been reduced to half price.' – 'Then get there very early. It's a case of _____ and the best bargains disappear within minutes.'
first come, first served

1 'I wonder if I'll ever get on with my new boss. She's always so bad-tempered.' – 'Don't worry, her _____ and her other staff seem to like her enormously.'

2 'I don't believe it! You mean old George Smith is getting married! But he's 76 years old!' – ' _____ and he won't have to live alone in that large house.'

3 Emma's love for John seems to have grown since he was transferred to the Australian office. You know what they say, _____ .

4 'I'm very sorry but I must admit a mistake in those calculations regarding the warehouse stock.' – 'I'm glad you have, _____ and we have plenty of time to rectify the situation.'

5 'Nigel's girlfriend may be very pretty but she's so selfish and makes him pay for everything.' – 'He'll learn that _____ .'

Exercise 113

Complete the sentences by choosing a suitable proverb.

Example
'We had a great time in the office last Friday. The boss was away so
we brought in some beer and had a little party.' – 'Obviously a case
of _____ !'
still waters run deep   when the cat's away the mice will play
when the cat's away the mice will play

1 'I'm worried about my brother. He went to Spain a month ago and I
   haven't heard a word from him.' – 'Oh, don't worry. Remember that
   _____ and I'm sure he's OK.
   a miss is as good as a mile   no news is good news

2 'He's had a terrible week. First he lost his season ticket, then his wallet
   was stolen and now he's broken his spectacles.' – 'Ah well, as the
   saying goes, _____ .'
   it never rains but it pours   actions speak louder than words

3 'Tony's been writing a dictionary for five years and he's depressed
   because it's taking so long.' – 'Tell him not to be too discouraged.
   _____ , as they say.'
   don't make mountains out of molehills   Rome wasn't built in a day

4 James has been offered the job of Services Manager but he doesn't
   think he has the necessary experience. I told him to _____ .
   strike while the iron's hot   do as he would be done by

5 'Can I borrow your car tomorrow, Steve? Mine's in for a service.' –
   'Yes, of course. After all, I had yours last weekend and _____ .'
   one good turn deserves another   it's never too late to mend

Exercise 114

Explain the meanings of the idioms in *italics*.

Example
'Bob's worried about the commuting if he gets that job at Halford's.' –
'But he hasn't had the interview yet! Tell him *not to cross his bridges
until he comes to them.*'
not to worry about things before they happen

1 'I think you are being too sensitive about Michael – he didn't ignore
   you at the party deliberately – I doubt if he saw you. You're *making
   mountains out of molehills.*'

2 Well, it's best to accept the reduced offer on the house if he has the
   cash and you want to sell it quickly. *A bird in the hand is worth two in
   the bush* and you'll need the cash to pay for your new flat.

3 'Molly said the accident wasn't her fault. She claims the speedometer
   wasn't working properly.' – 'Oh, well. *A bad workman always blames
   his tools.*'

4 'If you rush the report, Mr Harrison will only ask you to do it again.
   More haste less speed, I always say.'

5 Pete doesn't believe in nearly scoring a goal. He once said *a miss is as
   good as a mile.*

Key

1 1 on the cards 2 on edge 3 in the dark 4 in her element 5 on the level

2 1 in 2 at 3 on 4 off 5 on

3 on call, up to the mark, out of the question, at someone's beck and call, on the beat, in my line, off the map, on tour, on the dole

4 1 break the news 2 break the bank 3 break the ice 4 break fresh ground 5 broken the back of

5 1 caused great laughter in the audience 2 discovered some new facts, made some new facts known 3 make her fully realize 4 recall it 5 at the end of the line, in last position

6 1 come into force 2 came into fashion 3 come to light 4 came to a head 5 came down to earth

7 1 treat unfairly 2 cooked perfectly 3 producing excellent results 4 served the purpose 5 act as host

8 1 is no longer used 2 was very lucky 3 was unsuccessful 4 wasn't as good as I expected 5 be extremely eager

9 1 get hold of the wrong end of the stick 2 get a move on 3 got the sack 4 get down to brass tacks 5 have got out of bed on the wrong side

10 1 was the cause of 2 escape from them 3 snubbed me, treated me in an unfriendly manner 4 let out the secret 5 scold him

11 1 went to town 2 going to rack and ruin 3 going behind his back 4 go the whole hog 5 gone to his head

12 had a brush, had the cheek, has too many irons in the fire, have her sleep out, have it out with her, have other fish to fry, has had it

13 1 keep quiet 2 keep a job 3 defend her position 4 saying what must be done in an authoritative tone 5 praise him too much

14 1 keep your fingers crossed 2 keep up with the Joneses 3 keeps himself to himself 4 keep in touch 5 keep up appearances

15 1 make short work of them 2 makes heavy weather of something 3 made a beeline for 4 making himself felt 5 making a virtue of necessity

16 1 cooperate fairly with you 2 be second in importance after you 3 trifling with his feelings 4 makes clever use of his opportunities

5 doing something that gives him an advantage, doing what he would like you to do

17 1 trick you   2 teasing you by telling you something that was untrue   3 make a greater effort   4 does their fair share of the work   5 using his good connections with influential people

18 1 put him in the picture   2 putting the cart before the horse   3 put the screws on us   4 putting two and two together   5 put your foot down

19 1 see her for the last time   2 seeing only the good things about him   3 manage to draft   4 find out the exact situation   5 understand

20 1 jars my nerves   2 aimed at attracting him   3 never do anything brilliant   4 organize his own private affairs   5 started the trouble

21 1 stands a good chance   2 stand on ceremony   3 It stands to reason   4 stand her ground   5 stand clear of

22 1 take sides   2 taking down a peg or two   3 take a dim view of it   4 take the bull by the horns   5 takes it in good part

23 1 turned a deaf ear to   2 turned John's head   3 turn over a new leaf   4 turned the corner   5 turned the scales in John's favour

24 stick at nothing, butters him up, blowing her own trumpet, picked holes in, asking for trouble, fly off the handle, tell her where to get off, rubs him up the wrong way

25 raining cats and dogs, pick a quarrel, leave much to be desired, meet you half-way, talk shop, harping on the same string, met his match, wears the trousers

26 1 burn his fingers   2 throwing his weight about   3 hold water   4 drives a hard bargain   5 throw cold water on one's plans

27 1 the journey   2 his cards   3 the air   4 a hint   5 his bluff

28 cutting it fine, kill two birds with one stone, let by-gones be by-gones, picked a quarrel, leads her a dog's life, cut me off with a penny

29 1 up   2 out   3 over   4 in   5 off

30 1 is in for   2 be down on   3 be on to   4 be at me   5 be up against

31 1 break her in   2 breaking in   3 break it up   4 break up   5 broken down

32 1 after   2 to   3 for   4 on   5 in

33 1 bring up   2 brought the deal off   3 brought it on   4 bring him round   5 bring up

34 1 calls for   2 call me up   3 call out   4 call for you   5 called on me

35 1 came up   2 coming along   3 came across   4 came to   5 come through

36 gone down with, fall back on, come up with, get on to, break out in,

dropping out of, come out with

37 1 down   2 off   3 through   4 in   5 over

38 1 getting at   2 got over   3 get along   4 get on   5 got through

39 1 go off   2 go over   3 go about   4 go into   5 gone off

40 1 keeping in with   2 make up for   3 put in for   4 burst in on   5 go through with

41 1 at   2 for   3 upon   4 in   5 to

42 1 kept at   2 keep on   3 kept you up   4 kept up   5 keep up with

43 1 looked over   2 look on   3 look down on him   4 looking into   5 look me up

44 1 hold off   2 holding information back   3 hold out   4 hold out for   5 hold over

45 of, out, off, over, up, on, to

46 1 to   2 about   3 over   4 on   5 in

47 1 make out   2 making things up   3 made over   4 made off   5 make it out

48 1 off   2 in   3 up   4 down   5 off

49 1 putting up   2 put you up   3 put you out   4 put it off   5 put up with

50 1 walk off with   2 take up with   3 run up against   4 walked out on   5 sending away for

51 1 have an empty petrol tank, have used all the petrol up   2 duplicate   3 read quickly   4 encountered   5 control you

52 1 set off   2 set back   3 set up   4 set her up   5 set about

53 1 in   2 off   3 on   4 down   5 out

54 1 taking off   2 take up   3 take after   4 taken in   5 taking on

55 1 turn up   2 turned down   3 turn out   4 turn away   5 turn him over

56 1 be drop-outs   2 do the washing-up   3 get further feedback   4 had a breakdown   5 given me the brush-off

57 1 delay   2 bursts   3 mistakes   4 written review   5 examinations

58 1 His story isn't borne out by the facts.   2 I'm very annoyed. I don't like being got at by people whom I hardly know.   3 The matter will be held over by the chairman until the next meeting on May 22nd.   4 Hardly anyone knew about the takeover. It had been hushed up successfully by the management.   5 Is that customer being attended to?

59 1 put on   2 turn it down   3 come back   4 take them on   5 rung off

60 1 live it down   2 work on him   3 tell on him   4 hunt them up   5 turned it down

61 1 get it through   2 get it round   3 saw through him   4 passed over

it   5 get it off

62 1 turns her on   2 seen through him   3 turn on me   4 get it
    through   5 see you through

63 open an account, current account, draw money out, deposit account,
    the bank rate, fill it in, crossed cheque, open cheque, a joint account,
    bounce, dishonour a cheque, pay in

64 shop around, set up shop, have goods on approval, pay cash, use
    hire-purchase, cut-price, puts them up, brings them down, pay
    through the nose, buy in bulk, selling like hot cakes

65 passed away, playing havoc with his health, looked washed out,
    shake it off, gone down with, running a temperature, be laid up,
    pushing up the daisies, feeling himself, taken a turn for the better

66 globe-trotter, chartered flights, scheduled flights, first class, economy
    class, go on holiday, go on a cruise, made a world-trip, live out of a
    suit-case, five-star hotels, travel light, boarding-pass

67 go camping, thumb a lift, bed-and-breakfast, stay the night, sleeping
    in the open, package holiday, coach-parties, holiday-makers, guided
    tour, put up at a hotel, pitch the tent, break camp

68 had an accident, write-off, no-claims bonus, rush-hour, stuck in a
    traffic jam, pulled in, turned on the engine, backing out, jammed on
    the brakes, ran into

69 in top, had a smash, a write-off, the bonnet, the boot, the motorway,
    put your foot down, test-drive, run in

70 getting through, phone-box, out of order, the ringing tone, gone
    dead, the line was engaged, a crossed line, hold the line, take the call,
    were cut off, bad line, ring off

71 on night-shift, working overtime, put in for a rise, a work-to-rule,
    came out on strike, black-leg, a picket line, white-collar workers, a
    lock-out, go on the dole

72 1 bee   2 cat   3 horse   4 donkey   5 dogs

73 1 kill two birds with one stone   2 have butterflies in my stomach
    3 got it from the horse's mouth   4 made a pig of himself   5 gets up
    with the lark

74 1 spend less money   2 he isn't as bad as he sounds   3 directing your
    wishes at the wrong person   4 protect her   5 check his activities,
    limit his possibilities

75 1 black   2 blue   3 white   4 grey   5 yellow

76 1 red herrings   2 red tape   3 a bolt from the blue   4 in his black
    books   5 black sheep

77 1 good at gardening   2 celebrated noisily in public   3 thinking
    deeply about something   4 an important occasion   5 a useless and
    troublesome possession

78 1 fall on his feet   2 wet behind the ears   3 make a clean breast of
it   4 keeping him at arm's length   5 racking my brains
79 1 keep your fingers crossed   2 keep your hair on   3 keep his hand
in   4 lose face   5 put their backs into it
80 1 in the nick of time   2 time after time   3 biding his time   4 for the
time being   5 doing time
81 1 am pressed for time   2 wasting time   3 in time   4 in no time
5 time flies
82 the morning after the night before, once in a blue moon, night-owl,
keep regular hours, a nightcap, an unearthly hour, is working nights,
getting on in years, at any moment
83 1 come to a dead end   2 cut me dead   3 a dead end   4 went
dead   5 is dead against
84 1 I'm flat broke   2 went flat out   3 fell flat   4 in a flat spin
5 that's flat
85 1 permanently   2 it's a good thing   3 is valid   4 say something
favourable about me   5 often
86 1 am hard up   2 take a hard line   3 a hard and fast rule   4 been
hard hit   5 be hard pressed
87 1 high and low   2 been in high spirits   3 be for the high jump
4 get on his high horse   5 high and dry
88 1 has been ill   2 thinks he is inferior   3 are scarce   4 an
unconvincing excuse   5 bad work
89 1 short change   2 made short work of   3 on short time   4 for
short   5 fell short of
90 1 lays it on thick   2 as thick as thieves   3 in thick with   4 vanished
into thin air   5 a bit thick
91 1 went off the deep end   2 got hold of the wrong end of the stick
3 in the end   4 odds and ends   5 make both ends meet
92 1 shooting a line   2 along the right lines   3 take the line of least
resistance   4 toe the line   5 all along the line
93 1 I've almost decided   2 you said frankly what you think   3 I am
inclined   4 she's worried about something   5 I'm unable to decide
94 1 stretch a point   2 get to the point   3 see the point of   4 what's
the point   5 in point of fact
95 1 have it both ways   2 out of the way   3 have her own way   4 on
the way out   5 went out of their way
96 1 get a word in edgeways   2 word for word   3 have a word
4 take his word for it   5 keeps her word
97 1 under any conditions   2 she resembles Karen very strongly   3 be
successful in job and social standing   4 lost her social and financial
position   5 are very important, mean very much

98 1 high and mighty   2 cut and dried   3 rough and ready   4 short and sweet   5 high and dry

99 1 heaven and earth   2 life and soul   3 wear and tear   4 body and soul   5 skin and bone

100 a stag-party, a confirmed bachelor, a hard drinker, a soft spot, a blind date, a chance meeting, seventh heaven, second thoughts, cold feet, Dutch courage

101 1 a tough customer   2 a close thing   3 a near thing   4 a big shot   5 a tight squeeze

102 1 a flying visit   2 a rolling stone   3 an open secret   4 plain sailing   5 an inside job

103 a cog in the machine, the gift of the gab, the tricks of the trade, the ins and outs, the lion's share, not trust him an inch, a bed of roses, ups and downs, the crack of dawn, a fish out of water, the pros and cons

104 1 the root of all evil   2 castles in the air   3 a skeleton in the cupboard   4 a smack in the eye   5 a storm in a tea-cup

105 1 on behalf of   2 at the rate of   3 in response to   4 in exchange for   5 in contact with

106 1 on the point of   2 in view of   3 in want of   4 in possession of   5 in favour of

107 1 once or twice   2 on and on   3 on and off   4 up and about   5 by and large

108 1 as fit as a fiddle   2 as pale as a ghost   3 as deaf as a post   4 as quick as lightning   5 as warm as toast

109 1 as clear as a bell   2 as good as gold   3 as bold as brass   4 as white as a sheet   5 as old as the hills

110 1 eats like a horse   2 smokes like a chimney   3 goes like a bird   4 drinks like a fish   5 fit like a glove

111 1 a fish out of water   2 a memory like an elephant   3 like a red rag to a bull   4 a hide like a rhinoceros   5 eyes like a ferret

112 1 bark is worse than her bite   2 better late than never   3 absence makes the heart grow fonder   4 honesty is the best policy   5 beauty is only skin deep

113 1 no news is good news   2 it never rains but it pours   3 Rome wasn't built in a day   4 strike while the iron's hot   5 one good turn deserves another

114 1 treating the matter with too much importance   2 a thing which is certain now is better than a risk later   3 an incapable person always puts the blame on the instruments at his disposal, never on his own lack of skill   4 the more you hurry, the more time you lose by making mistakes   5 failure is failure, however close you were to success